A MANUAL OF BEDFORDSHIRE LACE

Christine Sprigett   considers Brok a better thread

Threads for Bedfordshire

50 R D'Alsace   = 100/3 Brok
30   "   = 36/2 Brok = 150 Cordonet Special

PAM ROBINSON

A MANUAL OF
BEDFORDSHIRE LACE

RUTH BEAN
Carlton, Bedford

Published by Ruth Bean, Victoria Farmhouse, Carlton, Bedford MK43 7LP, England.

Distributed in the USA by Robin & Russ Handweavers, 533 North Adams Street, McMinnville, Oregon 97128, USA.

ISBN 903585 20 0

Photography, Miles Birch, North Bedfordshire Borough Council.
Designed by James Skelton.
Typeset by Pro-Arts, Wellingborough.
Printed in Great Britain at the University Press, Cambridge.

Acknowledgements
The author and publishers wish to acknowledge help received during preparation of this book: from Mrs Eunice Arnold who made valuable suggestions on the text, from Mrs Maria Rutgers who drew the diagrams and from Mr Miles Birch who photographed the lace.

Contents

PART III. WORKING NOTES FOR THE PATTERNS

Other techniques

Introduction

Background

Now usually referred to as 'Bedfordshire', this lace was originally known as 'Bedfordshire Maltese'. Its origin in England, around 1850, was due to the need for English lace-makers to compete with the popular lace being imported from Malta and with the machine-made laces appearing on the market in large quantities. It could be made much more quickly than the finer point ground lace.

Nineteenth century Maltese lace developed from the lace of Genoa. The designs incorporated decorative circles, groups of leaves, whole stitch trails (narrow bands of weaving) and the distinctive Maltese Cross. The repetitive designs were made all in one piece with plaited bars forming the ground and linking together other sections of the lace. The headside was made in plaited bars too, usually in the traditional arrangement called ninepin. It was made in thick silk threads rather than the fine flax of the older Genoese lace. Maltese lace was popular for collars, cuffs, and shawls; the last of these was made by joining together strips several inches wide.

Bedfordshire Maltese copied this general style of design, retaining the whole stitch trails, the ninepin edge, the plaited bars with picots, circles and leaves. It too was made all in one piece but had no Maltese Cross. The leaves were usually square-ended rather than pointed, and it was made mainly in white cotton instead of silk. The name 'Bedfordshire' now indicates a type of lace though it was made throughout the East Midlands.

How to use the book

As with other laces there are general methods for working Bedfordshire lace, but as the designs are freer than in Torchon lace the general rules need to be adapted to suit the particular pattern being worked. There can be more than one way of working certain parts of the pattern.

In Part I notes are set out to guide the beginner through the basic lace-making materials, techniques and the working of a practice band of stitches. This is followed by a general introduction to the parts of a Bedfordshire pattern, with guidance on starting and finishing the lace. The information in this section may seem technical but the lace-maker will find it useful to refer to later in the course.

Part II comprises 14 Bedfordshire lace patterns specially designed for this course, with working instructions. They are arranged in order of complexity. Every pattern is an exercise in one or more techniques of Bedfordshire lace and is intended to advance the lace-maker a step further. Pattern 14 makes use of the experience gained in this course.

Part III contains Working Notes Nos 1–20 which are given in a separate booklet in the back pocket. These working notes describe in detail the techniques required for the working of specific points in the patterns. They are referred to throughout the patterns (N1–20) though they too are introduced progressively, starting from the basic elements such as plaits and picots and ending with techniques such as crossing trails. These working notes apply not only to the patterns chosen for this course but also to the working of other Bedfordshire lace patterns.

Prickings for each of the patterns are also included. Finally a Glossary is provided where lace-making terms used in the book are explained. Every effort has been made to make this Glossary as comprehensive as possible so that beginners may find in it explanations for unfamiliar terms.

Part I

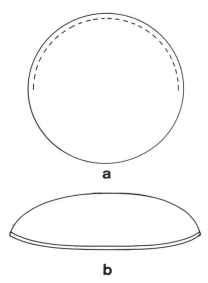

Figure 1
Lace pillow.
a. Calico bag with unstitched edge for insertion of board and straw.
b. Finished flat pillow.

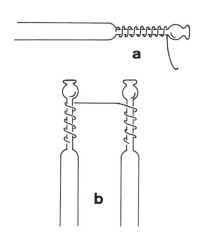

Figure 2
Winding bobbins.
a. 'Over-full' bobbin.
b. Pair of wound bobbins.

LACE-MAKING MATERIALS AND TECHNIQUES
The lace pillow

Several kinds of pillow are available from lace suppliers but for the beginner a simple round one is the easiest both to make and to support when working. The main requisite of a lace pillow is that it should be very hard and firm so that the pins stuck into it while making the lace will be firmly held in place. A first pillow can be made in the following manner (Fig 1).

Prepare a bag from two circular pieces of very strong calico, about 23 in (58 cm) in diameter. Insert a piece of plywood about 17 in (43 cm) in diameter into this bag. Push chopped straw into the bag on top of the plywood, a little at a time until it is packed as tightly as possible. The straw must be pushed in firmly all the time so that there are no air gaps inside. When it will hold no more straw sew the ends together. Trim the cloth to within ¾ in (2 cm) of the board and stitch it upwards round the edge.

A piece of dark blue or dark green cotton material should be placed over the top of the pillow and sewn neatly round the bottom edge.

It is important that this top material is cotton which will not 'fluff', to avoid pieces of fluff being worked into the lace.

Bobbins

Bobbins are the lace-maker's tools. These are traditionally made in wood and bone but today can also be found in plastic. They have a shank which is held when working, a long neck on which the thread is wound and a short neck on the head where the thread is hitched. The ring of beads at the bottom end, called a spangle, adds weight to the bobbin and helps keep the correct tension on the thread.

Bobbins work in pairs joined together by the thread.

Threads

Thread used for lace-making is usually cotton or linen and comes in many makes and sizes. The choice of thread depends on the distance between pin-holes of the pattern being worked and the use to which the lace will be put. The threads used to make each pattern in the book are indicated and these provide a general guide. The following may serve as a further rough guide:

Pinholes $1/16$ in (2 mm) apart on the footside and trail – DMC 50.

Pinholes $1/16$–$1/8$ in (2–3 mm) apart – Campbell's linen 100, Bocken's linen 90 or B.O.U.C. linen 100.

Pinholes $5/32$ in (4 mm) apart - Bocken's linen 80 or DMC 30.

Winding a pair of bobbins

The thread is wound clockwise onto one bobbin of the pair (Fig 2a). Wind enough thread onto it so that it is 'over full'. Wind thread from this first bobbin, clockwise, onto the second bobbin of the pair. The two bobbins will now look like those in Figure 2b and the thread has to be hitched onto the short neck at the top, to stop it from coming off.

1

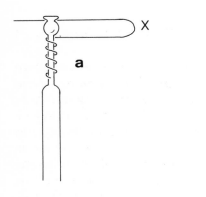

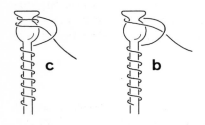

Figure 3
Hitching a thread.
a. Loop on the thread held at x.
b. One hitch.
c. Two hitches.

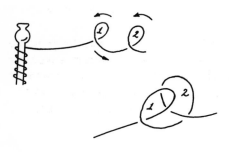

Figure 4
Fastening on a new thread.
Second loop is behind first.

Hitching a thread

Hold the bobbin and the thread in the left hand. Make a loop with the thread in the right hand, holding it at point x (Fig 3a). Wind the thread clockwise, two or three times round the groove in the neck of the bobbin (Fig 3b–c), i.e. round the front, to the back and back round again.

Pull on the thread making sure that as the hitch tightens it does not slip down onto the bobbin or off the neck.

Hitch the second bobbin of the pair in the same way.

Prickings

These are the patterns from which the lace is worked. They are made by pricking pin-holes into a piece of card using a needle held in a tool called a pin-vice. The card should be fastened down onto a cork tile with drawing pins and the pin-vice held in a vertical position to ensure the pricked holes are straight and accurate. A betweens needle size 8 is best as it does not make the pin-holes too large and it should protrude from the end of the pin-vice no more than $^3/_{16}$ in (5 mm). Guidelines are drawn on the pricking to show the working of some of the threads. These should be drawn in with pen and indian ink or a very fine felt-tipped pen.

Dressing a lace pillow

The pattern is pinned onto the pillow at the corners. The pins should be pushed right down into the pillow. A cloth is then placed over the card so that only 2 or 3 in (7.5 cm) of the pattern show. This cloth, called a cover cloth prevents the bobbins from catching on the card. It should be about 9 in by 15 in (22 x 38 cm), hemmed and made from non-fluffy material in a dark green or blue. Cotton material is best. The dark colours are more restful for the eyes during work.

Setting up the lace

This means moving the lace up the pattern in order to increase the length being worked, or to turn round the next corner.

Wrap the bobbins tightly in the cover cloth. Make it into a bundle by pinning the cloth. Move the bundle up slightly so that the threads on the bobbins are slack. Pin the bundle down onto the pillow, the important thing being not to let it slip, or the weight will pull the lace and spoil it. Carefully remove all pins from the lace, then take out the pins holding the bundle onto the pillow. Do not remove pins holding the cover cloth around the bundle of bobbins. Lift the lace and bundle carefully into the position required to begin working again. Re-pin the lace to the pattern, pinning back at least two pattern repeats. Remove pins from the cover cloth, unwrap the bundle and lay out the bobbins ready to resume work.

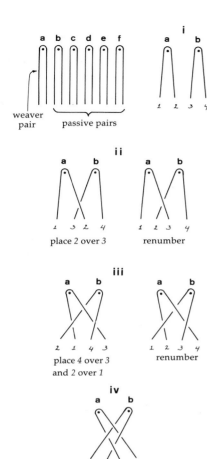

weaver pair   passive pairs

ii

place 2 over 3   renumber

iii

place 4 over 3 and 2 over 1   renumber

iv

place 2 over 3
weaver pair begins on the left

Figure 5
Making a whole stitch.

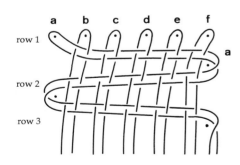

Figure 6
Whole stitch.

Fastening on a new thread

As bobbins run out of thread they need to be refilled and the new thread must be introduced into the lace (Fig 4).

When there are only about 8 in (20 cm) of thread left on the bobbin, unwind it and refill the bobbin. Set a pin at the edge of the pricking. Make two loops on the end of the new thread by moving the end away from you and back over itself towards you anti-clockwise. Make two loops in this manner and put the second loop behind the first one. Put both loops over the pin at the edge of the pricking. Pull the thread to tighten the loops round the pin. Take the old thread and wind it onto the bobbin with the new thread and make the hitch on the bobbin with both. Use both threads together until the new one is worked far enough to be securely anchored. Remove the old thread from the bobbin and leave it to the back of the pillow. Later, the pin holding the new thread hitch is removed. Hold the hitch down while removing the pin. When pins are removed from the lace these ends can be trimmed close to it.

THE STITCHES

As with other bobbin lace, Bedfordshire lace is based on simple weaving techniques involving the use of two stitches: whole stitch and half-stitch. Working the following practice band will allow the beginner to gain some experience in working these basic stitches.

Working the practice band

Whole stitch

Wind 6 pairs of bobbins in DMC 30. Use the braid practice pattern (Pricking A) and hang one pair on each of pins *a*, *b*, *c*, *d*, *e* and *f*. Begin by working from left to right with pairs *a* and *b* (Fig 5i). The threads are numbered from the left.[1]

★With the left hand place thread 2 over thread 3. Renumber threads from the left (Fig 5ii).

Using both hands simultaneously place: thread 4 over the new thread 3 and thread 2 over thread 1. Renumber from the left (Fig 5iii).

With the left hand place thread 2 over thread 3. This completes one whole stitch (Fig 5iv).★

Row 1. Pair *a*, the weaver pair, has moved through one pair, the passive pair *b*, to the right. The passive pair *b* remains on the left and the weaver pair works through the next pair *c* to the right. Make the movements ★ to ★ with the weaver pair and the next pair. Leave the passive pair *c* on the left. Take the weaver pair through the next pair *d* to the right. Leave the passive pair *d* on the left.

---

[1]Short sections of text which may need to be referred to elsewhere are defined between stars (★) or bullets (●) or daggers (†).

3

Work the weaver pair through the passive pairs *e* and *f* (Fig 6). The weaver pair is twisted once, right thread over the left, and is now on the right-hand side. Put up a pin between the last pair worked through, *f*, and the weaver pair. The weaver pair *a* should be on the right-hand side of the pin and the last passive pair worked through, *f*, on the left of it (Fig 7i).

Row 2. The weaver pair now works row 2 (Fig 6) in whole stitch from the right-hand side, back to the left. The movements are exactly the same as before. The threads are numbered from the left (Fig 7i). Work the movements ★ to ★ above, with the weaver pair *a* and the passive pair *f*, making a whole stitch in front of the pin. This whole stitch encloses the pin. A pin is enclosed by working a stitch in front of it with the same two pairs which worked the stitch behind it. See Fig 7ii–iv.

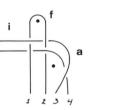
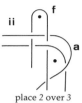

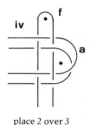

Figure 7
Starting a new row; details for Fig 6.

Weaver pair *a* has now moved through one passive pair *f* to the left. Leave the passive pair on the right. Take the weaver pair through the next pair *e* to the left. Leave the passive pair *e* on the right. Work through until the weaver pair is on the left-hand side. Put up pin between the weaver pair and the last pair worked through. Weaver pair *a* will be on the left of the pin and the passive pair *b* will be on the right of the pin. Twist the weaver pair once, right over left. To work row 3 (Fig 6) take the weaver pair back through the passive pairs to the right-hand side.

Work rows of whole stitch until you feel you have gained some competence. Remember the movements are the same, counting the threads from the left, whether working to the left or right.

When you have completed several rows, twist each of the passive pairs once and continue the braid in half-stitch. Begin with weaver pair *a* on the left-hand side.

Half-stitch

With the same number of bobbins continue the practice band. The threads are still numbered from the left (Fig 8).

    i. (Fig 8i) Place thread *2* over thread *3*. Renumber.

    ii. (Fig 8ii) Place thread *4* over *3* and thread *2* over *1*. Stop.

Repeat these movements with the next pair to the right. Continue to work across the pairs until the weaver pair is on the right-hand side. Note that only one thread of weaver pair *a* has worked across the braid. Set the

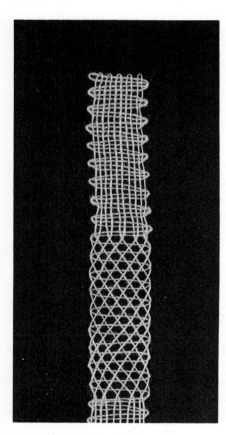

Plate A
Practice band.

4

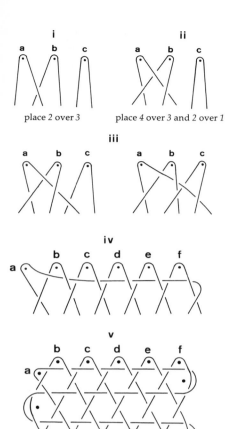

i

place 2 over 3

ii

place 4 over 3 and 2 over 1

iii

iv

v

Figure 8
Half-stitch.

pin as before, between the weaver pair and the last pair worked through. There must be 2 threads on the right-hand side of the pin. Work back to the left-hand side making exactly the same stitch movements. Set the pin between the weaver pair and the last pair worked through making sure that there are 2 threads to the left of the pin. Gradually star-like shapes will begin to appear. Half-stitch is not very firm at the edge of lace so when some competence is gained in making the stitch, twist the weaver pair once more, right over left, before setting the pin. Note that all the pairs have one twist on them when working in half-stitch. Care should be taken when working half-stitch not to muddle the bobbins.

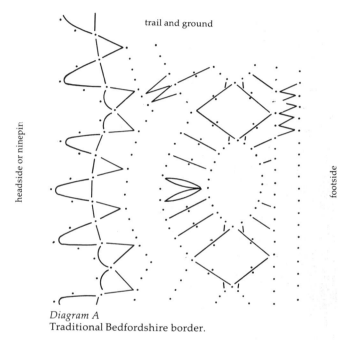

trail and ground

headside or ninepin

footside

Diagram A
Traditional Bedfordshire border.

GENERAL NOTES ON WORKING BEDFORDSHIRE PATTERNS
Sections of the lace, Diagram A

The following general notes introduce Bedfordshire patterns, describe their main features and provide general guidelines on starting, working and finishing the lace. A traditional design for a rectangular border has been chosen to illustrate the points. In Part II the student will find specific instructions on setting in, working and finishing the lace for each of the 14 patterns.

For the purpose of setting in (starting) the lace, the pattern is divided into three sections (see Diagram A): the outer left-hand edge, often referred to as the headside or ninepin; the centre section which includes the trail and the ground; and the outer right-hand edge, which is called the footside. Some of the sections are worked together as will be seen in the patterns themselves.

5

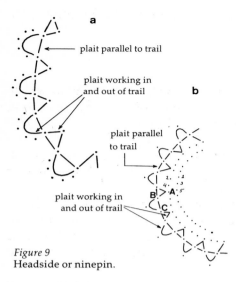

Figure 9
Headside or ninepin.

a
plait parallel to trail
plait working in and out of trail
b
plait parallel to trail
plait working in and out of trail

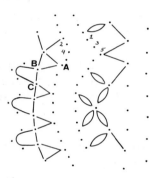

Figure 10
Trail and ninepin. Guide to setting in. for the trail.

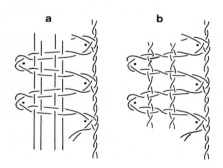

Figure 11
Footside.
Guide to setting in.
a. Whole stitch passive pairs.
b. Twisted passives.

The headside

In Bedfordshire lace the headside is usually called the ninepin (Fig 9). This is a distinctive arrangement of plaited pairs around the outer edge, with and without picots (decorative loops).

The term ninepin does not describe a technique in itself but rather a system of plaited pairs working in and out of the trail – passing through plaited pairs running parallel to the trail (see Fig 9a–b).

The number of picots on the plaits is usually an odd number; 3, 5 or 7. They are usually on the outer plait giving it the appearance of an elongated oval, but they can be found on the plait running parallel to the trail as well (Fig 9b).

There are other arrangements of plaited pairs around the headside of Bedfordshire lace; in some older patterns there may be several plaited pairs working in and out of the trail.

Instructions for setting in and working the ninepin are given in Pattern 4 while other headside arrangements can be found in Patterns 8, 9, 10 & 12.

Trails and ground

Trails are worked with a weaver pair and several pairs of passives; the number of passives will depend on the thread size and the width of the trail. The trail is usually worked in whole stitch but can be worked in half-stitch.

Pairs for the plaited headside and for plaits or leaves in the ground are set into the trail as the work progresses. At pins on the trail where no pairs enter or leave, the weaver pair is twisted once before setting the pin.

Figure 10 shows a typical border pattern with the setting in pin-holes indicated: 1, 2 and 3 for the trail; A, B and C for the ninepin.

Full instructions for setting in and working the trail and ninepin are given in Pattern 4 and these can also be followed when working other patterns.

The footside

The footside has an edge pair and a weaver pair, both of which are always twisted (Fig 11). The number of twists depends on the thread size and the spacing between pin-holes, but usually the weaver pair is twisted once and the outer edge pair twice or three times.

In the patterns of this book the edge pair is to be twisted three times unless stated otherwise.

Inside the footside pins, running parallel to the edge of the lace for its whole length, are footside passive pairs, usually two. The passive pairs may be worked in whole stitch (Fig 11a) or they may be twisted (Fig 11b). If they are twisted the weaver pair is also twisted in between each pair.

The footside weaver pair is twisted several times around inner pins at which no other pairs enter or leave; the number of twists depends on the thread size and the width of the footside. Three or four twists will probably suffice (see Fig 11b).

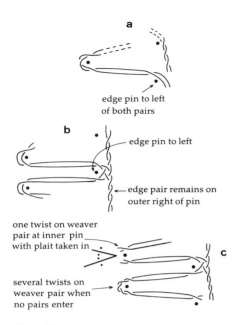

edge pin to left
of both pairs

edge pin to left

edge pair remains on
outer right of pin

one twist on weaver
pair at inner pin
with plait taken in

several twists on
weaver pair when
no pairs enter

Figure 12
Edge pins.

Figure 13
Guide to setting in a border.

Pairs for plaits or leaves in the ground can be set into the inner pin-holes of the footside.

Edge pins

Edge pins are worked with the weaver pair and the edge pair, in whole stitch and twists. They are then enclosed in the special way described below. The usual way of enclosing a pin is given on p. 4.

The edge pin is put up to the *Left* of *Both* pairs (Fig 12a).

Work the weaver pair to the right-hand side through the passive pairs. Twist it once. Put up the edge pin to the *Left* of it, i.e. between the weaver pair and the last pair of passives worked through.

Now work a whole stitch with the weaver pair and the edge pair. Twist the right-hand pair three times and the left-hand pair once. The edge pin is now on the *Left* of *Both* pairs. The right-hand pair remains on the outer right-hand side of the edge pin to become the edge pair for the next edge pin (see Fig 12b).

The left-hand pair becomes the weaver pair to the next inner pin of the footside and works back through the passive pairs. As it works back across the passive pairs it travels in front of the edge pin and this move-ment encloses that pin (see Fig 12c).

Full instructions for setting in and working the footside with whole stitch passive pairs are given with Pattern 6; for twisted passive pairs in Pattern 7, and these can be followed when working other patterns.

Points to consider before setting in a border

Basic instructions for setting in and working the trail and ninepin are given in Pattern 4; for the footside in Patterns 6 and 7.

Fig 13 is an example of a typical border pattern. Before beginning work, it is essential to consider the finished required size of the lace and the number of pattern repeats which will be needed down each side before the corner is turned. This may seem obvious but can be particularly important if the lace is to be attached to the outer edge of a hemmed piece of linen such as a handkerchief or table-cloth.

Check that a full pattern repeat will fit at the end of one side before the corner is turned. The repeats may be either too long or fall just short of the corner. Consider making alterations to the design in the corner but if this is not possible the only alternatives are either to choose another pattern or to mount the lace onto the linen, using the three-sided stitch (described on p. 11) instead of attaching it to the other edge.

Begin a border two or three pattern repeats from the first corner so that, should you decide to make each side shorter than originally intended, it will still join together.

Study the whole pattern carefully, especially the trail, before deciding where to begin. The setting in point is also the finishing point and this is important for fastening off the pairs. The more plait and leaf pairs that can

7

be taken up into the trail before setting the last pins the better, and the easier it is to dispose of threads. See also the section on finishing below, and on removing pairs (N15).

Decide where to begin the trail after noting the points at which plaits, leaves and the ninepin edge, enter and leave it. If possible try to avoid setting in the trail at these points but choose pin-holes which are set simply as trail pins. For example, in the border pattern given here (Fig 13) the best place to begin the trail would be at the pin-hole marked 1. No pairs enter or leave at the first three pin-holes. While setting in, the ninepin can begin at pin A: the plait and leaf pairs of the ground are not set in until trail pins 5, 8 and 14 are worked.

Choosing this place to begin also means an efficient use of pin-holes when the border is completed and the finished lace is joined into the starting pin-holes. There will be a need to accommodate pairs from the plaits E and F, for example. These pairs can be taken into the trail quite easily as the last pin-holes are being worked. Pairs from the trail are removed to accommodate them (see N15) leaving only the original number of passive pairs to fasten off into the loops left on the pin when the lace was begun (N7).

The ninepin almost always fastens out into the trail that is already made and this is also true for our particular example where the pairs from plait G would fasten off into the trail already made.

FINISHING THE LACE

If, as shown here, the lace you have worked is a border, set the first repeats of the pattern back onto the pricking making sure that the lace is not twisted over itself.

All pins of the first repeat, more if the repeat is a short one, must be placed in the pin-holes and pushed down into the pillow to hold the lace firmly in place. When the lace is not a border pattern, e.g. a motif, the pins at the beginning of the pattern should be pushed down into the pillow.

Where the lace finishes

The pairs fasten off into the pin-holes they would work to if the lace were to continue, i.e. into the starting pin-holes.

On the diagram (Fig 14), the starting pin-holes have been numbered 1 to 7. The lace fastens off into the starting pin-holes in the following way:

At the footside

The weaver pair and the edge pair fasten off into pin 5. The passive pairs fasten into the loops left on the pin when the lace was begun. For details see Note 7. The last leaf F fastens out into pin J.

At the trail

The weaver pair fastens off into pin 1. The passive pairs are fastened into

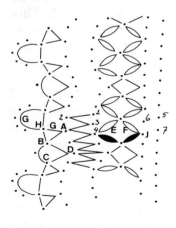

Figure 14
Finishing the lace.
The lace fastens out into starting pin-holes 1-7.

the loops left on the pin when the work was begun. Each pair fastens into its respective loop. It is important to watch that the loops are not muddled but are still lying in order (see N7), so that each passive is fastened into the correct loop.

Note. In patterns where extra pairs have entered the trail from leaves or plaits threads will have to be removed to accommodate these (N15), leaving only the same number of passive pairs as there are loops. If it is not possible to remove sufficient pairs before the last pin of the trail is reached, one extra pair may be kept in the trail and two pairs fastened into one loop.

The last leaf *E* fastens out into the trail at pin 4.

At the headside

The plait pairs *G*, which work from pin *H*, fasten out into pin *A* of the trail. The plait pairs from pin *H* meet the worked lace at pin *B* and are fastened into this pin-hole.

How to fasten off the pairs

The pins holding the finished lace in place are removed one at a time while the pairs are fastened into their respective pin-holes. The pins are replaced as the pairs are joined in, being finally removed only when all the pairs are fastened out and the bobbins have been cut off, leaving ends of thread long enough to pass into a needle to sew with. To do this two methods can be used.

Using a 0.6 mm fine crochet hook

Remove the pin from the lace. Put the hook through the lace pin-hole (Fig 15:1). Place the hook over the left-hand thread of the pair to be joined in (Fig 15:2). Pull this thread back through the lace pin-hole (Fig 15:3). This brings a loop of the thread through the pin-hole. Once you have a thread loop large enough to get the spangle of a bobbin through, remove the crochet hook but do not allow the thread to slip out of the lace.

Put the other bobbin of the pair, spangle first, through this loop of thread (Fig 15:4). Pull both threads down into the lace, replace the pin and push it back down into the pillow. Remove the next pin and join the next pair. Put the crochet hook through the lace pin-hole and pull the left thread of the pair through to make a loop, and so on until all the pairs are joined.

When fastening the trail or footside passive pairs into the loops left on the pins, release the loops one at a time. Put the crochet hook through the loop, pull the left-hand thread of the pair through and put the right-hand bobbin of the pair through the loop of thread as above. Pull the pairs down and release the next loop.

Strictly speaking lace should not have any knots in it, but beginners can find it difficult to control the threads when weaving them with a needle

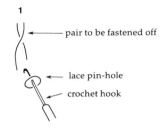

1
pair to be fastened off
lace pin-hole
crochet hook

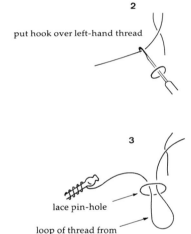

2
put hook over left-hand thread

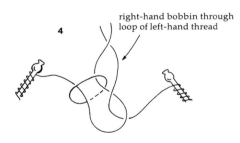

3
lace pin-hole
loop of thread from left-hand bobbin

4
right-hand bobbin through loop of left-hand thread

Figure 15
Finishing the lace with a crochet hook.

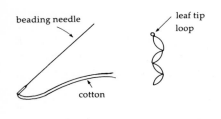

beading needle

leaf tip loop

cotton

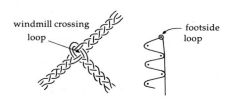

windmill crossing loop

footside loop

Figure 16
Finishing the lace with needle and thread.

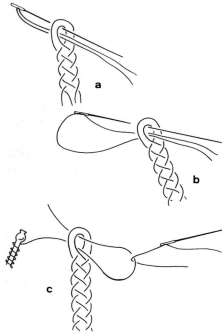

a

b

c

Figure 17
Finishing the lace with needle and thread; method of working.
a. Pass needle and cotton through lace pin-hole.
b. Make loop with cotton to pass bobbin through.
c. Thread loop from left-hand bobbin.

into the lace. It is therefore reasonable to put one knot on each pair to hold the threads until some experience is gained, particularly on plait and leaf pairs which can be pulled out of shape. Some lace-makers tie the pairs with reef knots to stop them from slipping loose.

Using needle and thread

This method is particularly useful when two pairs have to be fastened off into one pin-hole: the weaver pair and the edge pair on the footside, 2 pairs of a plait or leaf into a windmill crossing pin-hole or 2 pairs into the tip of a leaf (Fig 16).

Thread a piece of ordinary sewing cotton into a beading needle (more flexible than an ordinary needle). The point of the needle can be fastened into a pin-vice. Hold the ends of the cotton against the needle and push the needle, eye first, through the lace pin-hole (Fig 17a). This takes the cotton through the lace too. Open the cotton thread into a loop (Fig 17b). Put the left-hand bobbin of the pair to be fastened out through this loop of cotton, spangle first. Let go of the bobbin thread and pull the needle and cotton back through the lace pin-hole. As this is pulled through, the bobbin thread comes through too. Make a loop on the thread from the bobbin (Fig 17c) and remove the needle and cotton. Now pass the right-hand bobbin of the pair through the loop of thread from the left-hand bobbin (see Fig 15:4). Pull both threads down into the pin-hole and then repeat the procedure for the other pair that is to be joined into the same pin-hole. Replace the pin when both pairs are joined in.

Weaving thread ends into the completed lace

After removing the lace from the pillow, the ends of thread left from fastening out the pairs have to be carefully woven into the lace with a needle. The joining up and weaving in of ends can show if care is not taken. It is reasonable for beginners to leave the knots in the thread until some experience is gained, but then the knots can be undone one at a time before the threads are woven into the lace. Some lace-makers prefer to leave the knots in. The ends are woven only far enough to hold them securely and the excess thread is trimmed off close to the lace. The most difficult decision to make is where to hide the ends.

At the footside

Threads from the weaver pair, the edge pair, the passive pairs and any plait or leaf pairs fastened into the footside must be woven into the trail made by the footside passive pairs.

At the trail

Threads from the weaver pair, the passive pairs and any plait or leaf pairs that have been fastened into the trail are woven through the trail made by the passive pairs.

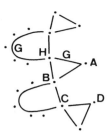

Figure 18
Method of weaving thread ends into
completed lace at headside (ninepin).

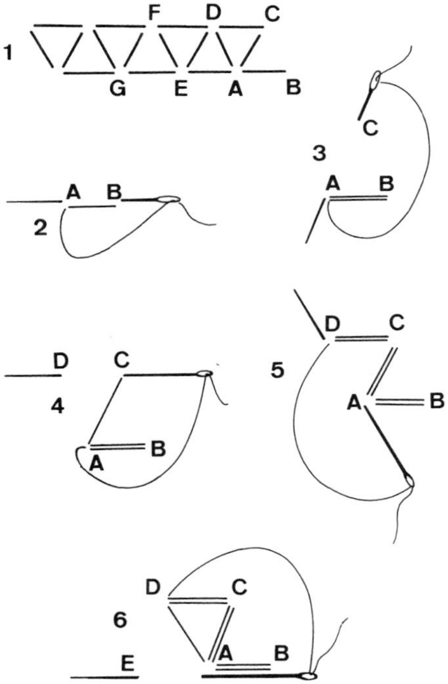

Figure 19
Mounting lace onto linen.
Three-sided punch stitch.
1. Completed row of stitches starting
from the right.
2-6. Working one triangle.

At the headside

In Bedfordshire lace the are usually some pairs which have to be woven into finished plaits or leaves. This is found particularly in the plaited headside. If the ends are not woven carefully the plaits or leaves can be spoiled: the following is one suggested method.

Follow Fig 18. After fastening out the pairs from pin H into pin-hole B there are 4 threads to dispose of. There are also 4 plaits radiating from pin B; H to B, A to B, and 2 plaits B to C. One thread can be woven into each of the four plaits. This is best done by taking the needle down through the plait, making a tiny stitch and bringing it back through again, and repeating this twice more. Some lace-makers prefer to tie these pairs in a reef knot and then simply trim close to the lace.

If the lace is a motif or a book-mark or is to be mounted in any way on backing material, the reverse side of which will not be seen, it is better not to weave ends into plaits or leaves at all. Instead tie the pairs in a reef knot against the pins as they are fastened out; cut off the bobbins and take the ends of thread through to the reverse side of the backing material. Tie the ends in a reef knot on the back and trim close.

Mounting lace onto linen

Plate B shows the three stages of mounting the lace onto linen.

The linen chosen should be of a suitable weight to match the thread of the lace. Most embroidery books give variations of hemming stitches but the most professional looking finish is achieved with a 3-sided punch stitch, although it is slow to work. The stitch is a row of triangles outlined in back-stitch, making a row of holes in the linen at the same time. A single thread can be pulled from the linen first which helps to emphasize the holes. Each stitch is worked twice. I find it better to use a thread finer than that which worked the lace, as the thicker linen threads tend to look very bulky if used to work this stitch. The thread should be pulled up firmly after each stitch.

Remember each stitch is worked twice, making double back-stitch into three holes of a triangle (Fig 19).

Bring the needle in at B and out at A – work back into B and out at A. Make a stitch from A to C and come back through A – work back into C and come up through D.

Make a stitch from D into C and back through D again. Make a stitch from D into A – back up through D; back into A and up through E. This is one complete triangle.

From E make a stitch back into A and up through E. Follow the triangle E to D and back to E, E to D and up through F, F to D and back through F, F to E and up through F, F to E and up through G. This completes the second triangle.

When the lace has been attached all the way round, the excess linen is trimmed from the back very close to the stitching. This stitch has the advantage of being very secure, enabling the linen to be trimmed without further hemming. It has the disadvantage of being very difficult to undo!

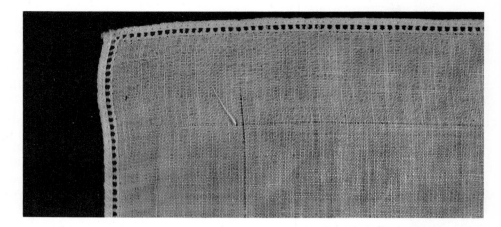

Plate B
Mounting lace onto linen.
Threads are pulled as a guide to the hemming.

The lace is secured by tacking and then with a three-sided punch stitch. Excess linen is trimmed from the back.

The finished item.

Part II

Pattern 1a

PATTERN 1a A BOOK-MARK

8 pairs of bobbins wound in DMC Brillante d'Alsace 30.

An exercise in making plaits with single picots set to the left and to the right. Crossing plaits by windmill crossing, the use of temporary pins, hanging pairs open round a pin, setting in new pairs.

Working notes (see Part III)

N1: Plaits.
N2: Single picots.
N8: Hanging pairs open round a pin.
N9a: Windmill crossing.
N9b: Setting in 2 new pairs into a plait by a windmill crossing.
N5: Temporary pins (marked ⊙) on the working diagram (Fig 20).

Setting in

★Set a pin in hole *a* and hang 4 pairs of bobbins open round it (N8). Starting from the right twist each pair once (see Fig 21). Use the outside right-hand pair as the weaver pair. Work the weaver pair in whole stitch through the other 3 pairs. Twist once and set pin *1* to the right of it. Work back to the right-hand side in whole stitch through the 3 pairs and leave the weaver pair on the right-hand side. Twist all 4 pairs once. With the 2 left-hand pairs from pin *1* work a plait to pin-holes *2* (Fig 20). At pin *2* set in 2 new pairs (N9b). Put a temporary pin in the hole marked ⊙ on the left, and hang 2 new pairs open round it (N8). With these two pairs and the 2 pairs of the plait, work a windmill crossing into pin-hole *2*. Follow N9a–9b to set in the 2 new pairs on the left. Leave the new pairs on the temporary pin and use the 2 left-hand pairs at pin *2* to make the plait to pin-hole *9*, working single picots into pins *3* and *4* on the left of the plait (N2a). Leave these 2 pairs at pin *9*. Remove the temporary pin and ease the 2 new pairs down round pin *2*. Make a plait with these 2 pairs to pin-hole *8*. When this plait is long enough lay these pairs, and the 2 pairs at pin *9*, to the left-hand side of the pillow.

Return to pin *a* and with the 2 pairs remaining there make a plait to pin *5*. At this pin 2 more new pairs are set in (N9b). Hang 2 pairs open round a temporary pin in the hole marked ⊙, on the right. With these 2 pairs, and the 2 pairs of the plait, work a windmill crossing into pin-hole *5* (N9a & 9b.ii: new pairs entering from the right). Leave the new pairs on the temporary pin and use the 2 right-hand pairs to make the plait to pin *10*, working single picots into pins *6* and *7* on the right of the plait (N2b). Remove the temporary pin and ease the new pairs down into the lace. Use these 2 pairs to make a plait from pin *5* to pin-hole *8*. Work a windmill crossing into pin-hole *8* with the 2 plait pairs from pin *2* and the 2 plait pairs from pin *5*.

After working the windmill crossing (at pin *8*) use the 2 pairs on the left of pin *8* to make a plait to pin *9*; with the 2 right-hand pairs work a plait

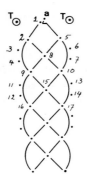

Figure 20
Pattern 1a. Guide to pin-holes.

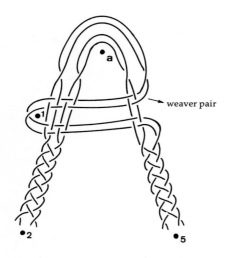

weaver pair

Figure 21
Working pins a & 1, 2 & 5.

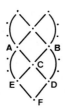

Figure 22
Finishing Pattern 1a.

to pin 10. At pin 9 work a windmill crossing with the pairs from pins 2 and 8. At pin 10 work a windmill crossing with the pairs from pins 5 and 8.★

Make a plait with the 2 right-hand pairs from pin 9 to pin 15. Then make a plait with the 2 left-hand pairs from pin 10 to pin 15. Work a windmill crossing into pin 15. With the 2 left-hand pairs at pin 15 make a plait to pin 16 and with the 2 right-hand pairs make a plait to pin 17.

With the 2 pairs remaining at pin 9 make a plait to pin 16, working left-hand picots at pins 11 and 12. Make a plait from pin 10 to pin 17 with the 2 pairs remaining at pin 10, working right-hand picots at pins 13 and 14. At pin 16 work a windmill crossing with the pairs from pins 9 and 15, and at pin 17 with the pairs from pins 10 and 15.

Continue the plaits, working picots on the outside plaits and windmill crossing each time 2 plaits meet at one pin-hole.

Finishing
★★Make plaits A to C, B to C; work windmill crossing at C; make the plaits from C to D and C to E. Make the plaits from A to E and B to D (Fig 22).

●Two plaits now meet at each of the pins E and D. After working the windmill crossings at pins E and D continue to use 2 threads as one and make plaits from E to F and D to F with these double pairs. The 8 pairs will meet at pin F. The plait is slightly more difficult to pull up. Work 2 half-stitches and then pull up, easing gently on single threads and the doubled threads, until it is firm and lying flat.●★★

Although they would not be used in a border to remove extra threads, these doubled plaits can give a pretty appearance to the end of a bookmark.

Figure 23
Working with doubled pairs from pins E & D to F.

Figure 24
Method of finishing Pattern 1a from pin F. Dividing bobbins into 3 bundles and making an ordinary plait.

End point, pin F, (Figs 23 and 24)
●●Refer to Plate 1a and Figs 23 and 24. The pairs are doubled up again. The 2 left-hand pairs (4 threads) from plait E make one thread A. The 4 threads of the right-hand pairs from E make one thread B. The 4 left-hand threads of plait D make one thread C and the 4 right-hand threads of plait D make one thread D. Work a windmill crossing into pin F: place the 4 threads B over the 4 threads C. Pass the 4 threads C over the 4 threads A

14

and threads *D* over *B*. Put up pin *F* and enclose it by passing the 4 threads *A* over the 4 threads *D*. ●● See Fig 24.

After setting pin *F* the bobbins can be grouped into 3 bundles (see Fig 24). Use the 3 bundles to make a braid (as hair is braided) at the bottom of the book-mark. When this is the desired length cross the 2 outside threads underneath the bundle and bring them back over the top. Tie a reef knot over the whole bundle and cut off all bobbins, leaving a tassel.

Two other ways of finishing the threads at the end of a book-mark are given elsewhere; one at the end of Pattern 1b, the other at the end of Pattern 3.

Pattern 1b

PATTERN 1b   A BOOK-MARK

8 pairs, wound in DMC Brillante d'Alsace 30.

An exercise in the techniques of Pattern 1a with the addition of leaves in the centre section and picots to the centre plaits.

Working notes (see Part III)

N1: Plaits.
N2: Picots.
N4: Leaves.
N8: Hanging pairs open on a pin.
N5: Temporary pins.
N9a: Windmill crossing.
N9b: Setting in 2 new pairs into a plait.

Setting in

Set in and work the pattern following instructions from ★ to ★ in Pattern 1a. See also Figs 20 & 21. After working the windmill crossing at pin *9* use the 2 right-hand pairs to make a plait to pin *17*, working a left-hand picot into pin *15* (N2). With the 2 left-hand pairs from pin *10* make a plait from pin *10* to pin *17*, working a left-hand picot into pin *16*. Work a windmill crossing into pin *17* (Fig 25).

With the 2 left-hand pairs at pin *17* make a plait to pin *20* and with the 2 right-hand pairs make a plait to pin *21*, working left-hand picots into pins *18* and *19*. With the 2 pairs remaining at pin *9* make a plait to pin *20*, working left-hand picots at pins *11* and *12* . Make a plait with the 2 pairs remaining at pin *10* to pin *21*, working right-hand picots at pins *13* and *14*.

Work windmill crossings at pin *20* with the pairs from *9* and *17* and at pin *21* with the pairs from *10* and *17*. Continue making the plaits with picots and working windmill crossings whenever two plaits meet. At pins *22, 23, 25* and *26* work picots on the right-hand side of the plait. At pins *24, 31* and *32* work windmill crossings.

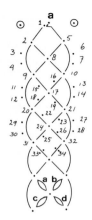

Figure 25
Pattern 1b. Guide to pin-holes.

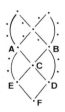

Figure 26
Finishing Pattern 1b.

In the next section, pins *33* and *34*, there are picots on both sides of the plait (N2c). Work a left-hand picot into pin *33*; work a half-stitch with both pairs and then make a right-hand picot on the opposite side of the plait. At pin *34* also work picots on both sides of the plait. Remember to work a half-stitch before making the second picot.

The centre section (Fig 25, *a,b,c* and *d*) is worked with 4 leaves (N4). Work leaves *a* and *b*; work a windmill crossing and then make leaves *c* and *d*.

Continue making the plaits with picots as necessary until pin-holes *A*, *B* and *C* are reached at the end of the pattern (Fig 26). Follow instructions from ★★ to ★★ for finishing as given in Pattern 1a. Also follow instructions ●● to ●● in Pattern 1a to work pin *F*.

Finishing

Finishing the threads

Continue by using 4 threads as one and make a plait in half-stitch to the desired length (Fig 27). Place all the bobbins in the centre of the pillow. Take the outside thread from the right and the outside thread from the left; pass them under the whole bundle of threads and bring them back over the top. They cross over beneath the bundle. Tie them in a reef-knot – left over right, right over left – over the bundle. Cut off all bobbins, leaving a tassel.

Figure 27
Method of finishing Pattern 1b from pin *F*

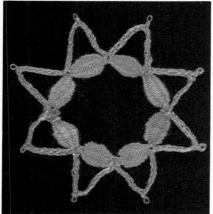

Pattern 2

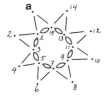

Figure 28
Pattern 2. Guide to pin-holes.

PATTERN 2   A SMALL MEDALLION MOTIF

Suitable for mounting in a brooch or pendant. It can also be used with Pattern 4 (which will be made separately) and mounted with it under the same frame or paper-weight.

4 pairs of bobbins wound in DMC Brillante d'Alsace 30.

An exercise in making leaves; working picots on the plaited pairs.

Working notes (see Part III)

N5: Temporary pins.
N8: Hanging pairs open on a pin.
N9c: Setting in 4 new pairs at one pin-hole.
N9a: Windmill crossing.
N10: Pinning pairs to the back of the pillow.
N4: Leaves.

Setting in

Set a temporary pin at *a* (Fig 28) and hang the 4 pairs of bobbins open round it (N8). Work a windmill crossing into pin *1* (N9a). Remove the temporary pin and ease the pairs down round pin *1*. Pin the 2 right-hand pairs to the back of the pillow (N10). With the 2 left-hand pairs make a plait to pin *2*, working a single left-hand picot into pin *2* (N2a). Continue to make the plait towards the left for a few half-stitches so that it is eased well up to pin *2* and the picot, before curving it round to the right to meet the leaf at pin *3*.

Return to pin *1* and release the 2 pairs that were pinned back. Use these 2 pairs to make a leaf to pin *3* (N4). Work a windmill crossing into pin *3* (N9a). Make a plait from pin *3* to pin *4* with the 2 left-hand pairs, working a left-hand picot into pin *4*. Continue towards the left for a few half-stitches before curving the plait round to pin *5*. Use the 2 right-hand pairs from pin *3* to make a leaf to pin *5*. Work a windmill crossing into pin *5*.

Continue working round the motif, making left-hand picots on the plaits into pins *6, 8, 10, 12* and *14* and working windmill crossings at pins *7, 9, 11, 13* and *15*. After setting pin *8* push all pins down into the pillow, otherwise it becomes awkward to make the leaves. Continue to push the pins down as the work progresses.

Finishing

Make the plait from pin *15* back to pin *1*, working a left-hand picot into pin *a*. Make the leaf from pin *15* to pin *1*. The 4 pairs meet and have to be fastened off into pin *1*. See section on finishing the lace, p. 8.

Push all the pins down into the pillow. Fasten off only 2 pairs into pin *1*, one pair from the plait and one pair from the leaf. Remove pin *1* and use the needle and cotton technique given on p. 10. Knot these 2 pairs once each. Knot each of the other 2 pairs in a reef knot. Cut off the bobbins, leaving ends of thread long enough to pass into a needle to sew with. Remove the pins and lift the lace. The ends of thread left can be taken through to the reverse side of the backing material. Tie them in a reef knot carefully so that the plait and leaf are not pulled out of shape, and then trim them off.

17

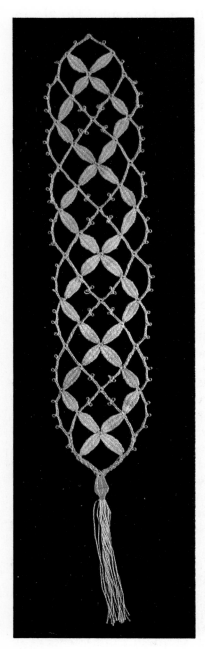

Pattern 3

PATTERN 3 A BOOK-MARK

12 pairs of bobbins wound in DMC Brillante d'Alsace 30.
An exercise in double picots and a review of the techniques learned so far.

Working notes (see Part III)
N8: Hanging pairs open.
N9a: Windmill crossing.
N5: Temporary pins.
N10: Pinning pairs to the back.
N3: Double picots.
N9c: Setting in 4 pairs at one pin-hole.
N9b: Setting in 2 new pairs into a plait.

Setting in
Hang 4 pairs of bobbins open on temporary pin *T* above pin *1* (N8) and Fig 29. Work a windmill crossing (N9c) into pin *1*. Remove temporary pin *T* and ease the pairs down round pin *1*. Pin the 2 right-hand pairs to the back of the pillow (N10).

With the 2 left-hand pairs make a plait to pin *3* working a double left-hand picot into pin *2* (N3). Set in 2 new pairs at pin *3* (N9a–b). Hang these pairs open on pin *T3*. Leave the 2 right-hand pairs on the temporary pin and with the 2 left-hand pairs make the plait to pin *5* working a double left-hand picot into pin *4*. Set in 2 more new pairs (as above) at pin *5* hanging them open round pin *T5*. With the 2 new pairs and the 2 plait pairs from pin *3*, work a windmill crossing into pin *5*. Leave the 2 right-hand pairs on the temporary pin and with the 2 left-hand pairs make the plait to pin *25*, working double picots on the left into pins *6*, *7* and *8*. Leave these 2 pairs ready to work pin *25*.

Return to the 2 pairs which were left on the temporary pin *T5*. Remove temporary pin *T5* and ease these pairs down round pin *5*. Make the plait to pin *17* and leave these 2 pairs here. Remove temporary pin *T3* and ease the 2 pairs down. Move these 2 pairs and the pairs for pins *17* and *25* to the far left of the pillow.

Return to pin *1*. Unpin the pairs left here and make a plait to pin *10*, working a double picot on the right-hand side into pin *9* (N3). Hang 2 new pairs on temporary pin *T10* and set these into pin *10* by a windmill crossing (N9a–b). Leave the 2 left-hand pairs on the temporary pin *T10* and with the 2 right-hand pairs make a plait to pin *12*, working a double picot on the right into pin *11*. Hang 2 more new pairs on temporary pin *T12* and set these in at pin *12*. Leave the 2 left-hand pairs on the temporary pin and make a plait with the 2 right-hand pairs to pin *24*, working double picots on the right-hand side into pins *13*, *14* and *15*. Leave these 2 pairs ready to work pin *24*.

Return to pins *12* and *10*. Remove the temporary pins and ease the pairs down. Make a plait from pin *12* to pin *18* and leave the 2 pairs ready to work pin *18*. Push pins down into the pillow out of the way.

18

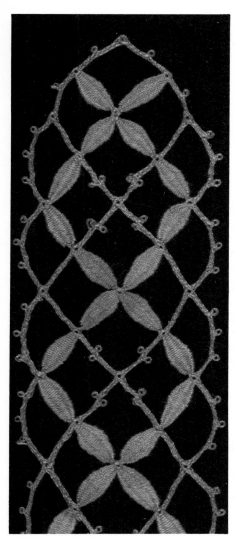

Detail for setting in.

Make the leaves (N4) from pin *3* to pin *16* and from pin *10* to pin *16*. Work a windmill crossing into pin *16* with the leaf pairs (N9a). Make the 2 leaves from pin *16* to pins *17* and *18* . Work windmill crossings into pins *17* and *18* with the plait and leaf pairs which meet at these pins (N9a).

With the 2 right-hand pairs from pin *17* make a plait to pins *19* and *20*. At these pins there are picots each side of the plait. Work the picot on the right into pin *19* – work one half-stitch with the plait pairs – work the picot on the left into pin *20*. Finish the plait to pin *23* and leave the pairs here. With the 2 left-hand pairs from pin *18*, make the plait to pins *21* and *22*. At these pins there are also picots set each side of the plait. Work the picot on the left into pin *21* – work one half-stitch – make the picot on the right into pin *22*. Finish the plait to pin *23*. Follow Note 3 to set double picots to the right and left.

Work a windmill crossing into pin *23* with the plait pairs. With the 2 left-hand pairs from pin *23*, make the left-hand plait to pin *28* working double picots into pins *26* and *27*. With the 2 right-hand pairs from pin *23* make the right-hand plait to pin *31*, working double picots into pins *29* and *30*. Leave these pairs at pins *28* and *31*. Push pins down into the pillow before continuing.

Return to pin *17* and make the leaf to pin *25*. Work a windmill crossing into pin *25* with the plait and leaf pairs that meet here. With the 2 left-hand pairs at pin *25* make the outer plait, with double picots set to the left, then make the leaf with the 2 right-hand pairs to pin *28*.

From pin *18* make the leaf to pin *24*. Work a windmill crossing into pin *24* with the leaf and plait pairs that meet here. With the 2 right-hand pairs at pin *24* make the outer plait, with double picots set to the right, then make the leaf with the 2 left-hand pairs to pin *31*. At pins *28* and *31* work windmill crossings with the plait and leaf pairs. Continue the pattern as far as pins *A* and *B* at the end. Do not forget to make a half-stitch between picots facing each other on either side of the centre plaits.

Finishing

Follow Fig 30. Work the windmill crossings at pins *A* and *B*. Two of the 4 pairs at each of these pins are no longer needed. Four threads can be removed and laid to the back of the pillow. Work the windmill crossing and then lay back the threads as shown in Fig 31. After laying back 4 threads each at pins *A* and *B* there will be only 4 threads left at each pin. Make the plaits *A* to *E* and *B* to *D*. Then make the leaves *C* to *E* and *C* to *D*. Work windmills at *E* and *D*. There are 4 pairs at each of these pins. Work plaits from pins *E* and *D* to pin *F* following instructions from ● to ● in Pattern 1a. Then work the windmill crossing at pin *F* following directions from ●● to ●● in Pattern 1a. Enclose pin *F* and unravel the twists from the threads. Bring all the bobbins together and then split them into three bundles. Keep 5 threads in each outside bundle and 6 threads in the centre bundle. Use this sixth thread as the weaving thread and with it weave under and over the 3 bundles as if making a leaf. Make this leaf into the

19

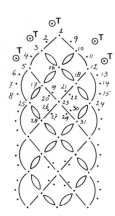

Figure 29
Pattern 3. Guide to pin-holes.

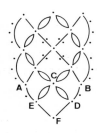

Figure 30
Pattern 3. Finishing the lace.

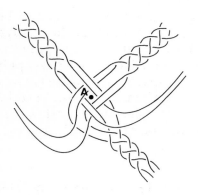

Figure 31
Removing 4 threads and laying them
to the back of the pillow.

desired length and then carefully lay the weaving thread with the whole bundle. Pass the outside thread from each side underneath the bundle, cross them over underneath and bring them back over the top. Tie these two threads in a reef-knot to hold all the threads together. Cut off the bobbins leaving a tassel.

Cut off the bobbins at pins *A* and *B* leaving long ends. Take the ends of the thread left here through to the reverse side of the mounting material using a needle. Tie in a reef-knot and trim.

20

Pattern 4

PATTERN 4   A CIRCULAR BORDER

It can be used successfully with the lace of Pattern 2 and mounted together under a frame or a paper-weight.

9 pairs, wound in DMC Brillante d'Alsace 30.

This is an exercise in working the trail and ninepin with practice in taking 2 pairs into one pin-hole where they leave immediately on the same side.

Working notes (see Part III)

Trail. Worked with a weaver pair and 4 pairs of passives in whole stitch.
N7: Hanging pairs in order on a pin.
N5: Temporary pins.
N13b.i: Setting in 2 new pairs into one pin-hole, on the left of the trail.
N13b.ii: Working 2 pairs into one pin-hole of the trail, leaving immediately on the same side.
   Ninepin. Worked with 4 pairs.
N9b: Windmill crossing to set in 2 new pairs into a plait.
N9a: Windmill crossing.
N2a: Picots set to the left of the plait.

Setting in the trail

Hang one pair of bobbins round a pin at *1;* this is the weaver pair (see Fig 32). Hang the passive pairs for the trail, in order from the right, on a temporary pin *T* above pin *1* (N7).

Working the trail

Take the weaver pair from pin *1* in whole stitch through the passive pairs. Twist the weaver pair once and put up pin *2* to its right. Enclose this pin by bringing the weaver pair, in whole stitch, back across the trail passives to pin *3*. Twist the weaver pair once and put up pin *3* to the left of it. Enclose this pin by taking the weaver pair back through the trail passives to pin *4*. Twist the weaver pair once and put up pin *4* to its right.

At this stage the temporary pin holding the passive pairs should be lifted, keeping the loops on it. Lay it behind pins *1* and *2*. Ease the passive pairs down into the trail (N7) and Fig 33. Enclose pin *4* by bringing the weaver pair back through the passive pairs to pin *5*. Twist the weaver pair once and put up pin *5* to the left of it. Enclose pin *5* by taking the weaver pair across the trail to pin *A*. At pin *A* (Fig 32) 2 new pairs are set in and 2 pairs left out to begin the ninepin plait. Do not twist the weaver pair at pins where plait (or leaf) pairs are to be taken in or left out of the trail.

Setting in the ninepin

● Follow N13b.i to set in 2 new pairs at one pin-hole. Hang the 2 new pairs open round temporary pin *S* above pin *A* (N8). With the weaver pair from pin *5*, work whole stitch through the 2 new pairs. Leave the weaver pair to the left of pin *A*, setting this pin between the two new pairs. Enclose pin

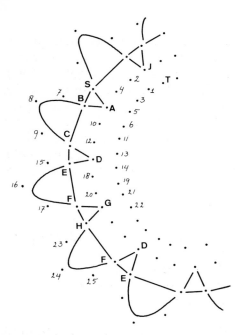

Figure 32
Pattern 4. Guide to pin-holes.

A with the left-hand new pair and bring it as the new weaver pair to pin *6*, working whole stitch through the right-hand new pair and on through the trail passive pairs. Twist the weaver pair once and put up pin *6* to the left of it. Leave the weaver pair and the trail at this pin. Remove the temporary pin and ease the 2 new pairs down into the lace at pin *A*. One of these pairs is the weaver pair at pin *6*, so ease it gently across the trail.●

Working the ninepin

●● The 2 pairs lying on the left-hand side of the trail at pin *A* are the 'old' trail weaver pair and the new right-hand pair. These 2 pairs are now used to make the plait to pin *B*. Two more new pairs are set into pin *B* to work the second plait of the ninepin (N9b). Put a temporary pin at *S* again and hang the 2 pairs open round it (N8). With these 2 pairs and the 2 pairs from plait *A-B* now work the windmill crossing into pin *B* (N9a-b). Leave the 2 right-hand pairs on the temporary pin and work the 2 left-hand pairs in a plait from pin *B* round to pin *C*. Work left-hand single picots into pins *7*, *8* and *9* while making this plait. After making the picot at pin *9* complete the plait to pin *C*. Leave these 2 pairs ready at pin *C* – return to pin *B* – remove temporary pin *S* and ease the 2 pairs down round pin *B*. Make the right-hand plait from pin *B* to pin *C* with these 2 pairs. This plait is made without picots. At pin *C* the 4 pairs from the two plaits meet and cross by a windmill into pin-hole *C* (N9a). Leave the two left-hand pairs at pin *C* and with the 2 right-hand pairs make the plait from pin *C* to *D* where it meets the trail. Leave the two plait pairs waiting at pin *D* and return to the trail at pin *6*.●●

Working the trail

★ Bring the weaver pair from pin *6* to pin *10* (Fig 32) – twist it once – put up pin *10* to its right. Work to pin *11* – twist the weaver pair once – put up pin *11* to the left of it. Work trail-pins *12* and *13*.★

Joining trail and ninepin

★★★ Bring the weaver pair from pin-hole *13* to pin *D*, do not twist it, do not put up pin *D*. Take the weaver pair through the 2 pairs of the plait in whole stitch. Leave the weaver pair to the left of pin *D*. Put up pin *D* between the two pairs of the plait. Enclose pin *D* with the left-hand plait pair by taking it as the new weaver pair in whole stitch through the right-hand plait pair and on through the trail passive pairs to pin-hole *14* (see N13b.ii). Twist the weaver pair once – put up pin *14* to the left of it. Leave the weaver pair and the trail at pin *14*.

Note. The left-hand pair of the plait at pin *D* becomes the new weaver pair for the trail. The 2 pairs now lying on the left-hand side of the trail are the 'old' weaver pair and the 'old' right-hand plait pair. These 2 pairs remain out at pin *D* to make the next plait in the ninepin.★★★

Each time the plait from the ninepin meets the trail at the equivalent of pin *D*, follow instructions ★★★ to ★★★.

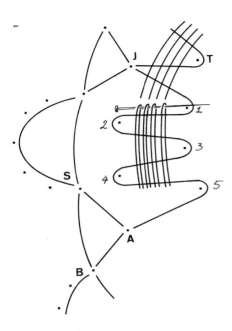

Figure 33
Finishing the lace of Pattern 4.

Return to the ninepin

★★ Return to pin *D* and make the plait from pin *D* to pin *E*, without picots. Use the 2 pairs waiting at pin *C* and make the left-hand plait from pin *C* to pin *E* without picots. Work a windmill crossing into pin-hole *E* (N9a). Leave the 2 right-hand pairs at pin *E*. With the 2 left-hand pairs make the plait from pin *E* round to pin *F* working left-hand single picots into pins *15*, *16* and *17* (N2a). Leave these 2 pairs at pin *F*. Make the right-hand plait without picots from pin *E* to pin *F*. Work a windmill crossing into pin-hole *F*. Leave the 2 left-hand pairs at pin *F* and with the 2 right-hand pairs make the plait from pin *F* to pin *G* where it meets the trail. Leave the plait pairs ready to work pin *G*.★★

Return to the trail

Return to pin *14* and work the trail-pins *18*, *19*, *20* and *21* and bring the weaver pair to pin *G*, as from ★ to ★ above.

Continue working the pattern in the following order.
1. Joining trail and ninepin – follow instructions ★★★ to ★★★.
2. Working the ninepin – follow instructions ★★ to ★★.
3. Working the trail – follow instructions ★ to ★.

Whenever 4 pairs meet at one pin-hole in the ninepin work a windmill crossing (N9a).

Finishing

Refer to Fig 33. Take the weaver pair from pin *T* and work the plait pairs into the trail at pin *J* as usual. Bring the left-hand plait pair as the weaver pair to pin *1*. This pair will fasten off into pin *1*. Finish the ninepin from pin *J* to pin *A* of the trail, working a windmill crossing into pin *S*. The 2 right-hand pairs from pin *S* make the plait to pin *A* and fasten into the trail at this pin. Follow the fastening off method, p. 10. With the 2 left-hand pairs from pin *S* make the plait to pin *B*. These 2 pairs fasten into pin *B*; again, use the above needle technique.

The passive pairs of the trail fasten off into the loops left on the pin when the lace was set in. Make sure the loops are not muddled but are lying in order. Use the crochet hook technique described on p. 9 to fasten off these pairs and the weaver pair. For the passive pairs begin the fastening off with the inside pair on the right of the trail and finish with the last pair on the left.

When all pairs are fastened off, leaving ends of thread long enough to pass through a needle, cut off the bobbins, remove the pins, lift the lace and weave in the thread ends as described on p. 10.

23

PATTERN 5   A MEDALLION

Can be mounted under a paper-weight or in a circular frame.
20 pairs of bobbins wound in Bocken's linen 80.

In this pattern a centre design is joined to the basic trail and ninepin described in the previous pattern. The centre design brings 4 sets of 2 single twisted pairs to meet the plait working the circle in windmill crossings. These pairs then form the leaves in the centre which cross in an 8-pair crossing. It is also an exercise in setting in single pairs (at each of the pin-holes marked *x*) to simplify working the centre, though this is not usual in Bedfordshire lace. Single pairs may be set into the remaining patterns but none of them actually work as single pairs.

Pattern 5

Working notes (see Part III)

Trail. Worked with 5 passive pairs and 1 weaver pair.
  Ninepin. Worked with 4 pairs.
  Centre motif. 10 pairs.
N5: Temporary pins.
N13a: Setting in 1 new pair.

24

N8: Hanging pairs open round a pin.
N9a: Windmill crossing.
N9b: Setting in 2 new pairs into a plait.
N4: Leaves.
N12: Crossing of 8 pairs.
N15: Removing extra pairs.

Setting in the trail
Refer to Fig 34. Hang the weaver pair on pin *1*, the 5 pairs of passives in order from the right on temporary pin *T* (N5), and work to pin *2* as in the previous pattern. Bring the weaver pair to pin *3* in whole stitch and set in 1 new pair. Follow Note 13a to set in the new pair. Take the weaver pair to pin *A* and leave it. Remove the temporary pin holding the new pair – ease the pair down into the lace at pin *3* and then leave this pair out at pin *3*. Lay it to the back of the pillow. Lift the temporary pin holding the trail passive pairs and lay this behind pins *1* and *2* with the loops on it.

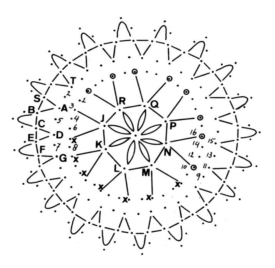

Figure 34
Pattern 5. Guide to pin-holes.

Setting in and working the ninepin
Two new pairs are set in at pin *A* (N13b.i). Bring the weaver pair from pin *3* to pin *A* and follow instructions ● to ●in Pattern 4 to set in the 2 pairs. Follow instructions ●● to ●● in Pattern 4 to work the ninepin to pin *D*. Work trail pins *4, 5* and *6* and then work to pin *D*.

Follow instructions ★★★ to ★★★ in Pattern 4 to work the trail and ninepin at pin *D*. Leave the weaver pair at pin *x* and follow instructions ★★ to ★★ in Pattern 4 to work the ninepin from pin *D* to pin *G*.

Set in 1 new pair at pin *x* following Note 13a, and work the trail pins *7* and *8*. Take in the pairs from the ninepin at pin *G* and continue to work the trail and ninepin until a new pair has been set in at each of the next six trail pins marked *x*. After setting in the last of these pairs there will be 8 pairs

25

out of the trail lying to the back of the pillow. Put the bobbins of the nine-pin and the trail passive and weaver pairs to the left of the pillow – out of the way.

Setting in and working the centre

Bring the 8 pairs left out of the trail to the front of the pillow and twist each pair 7 times. Hang 2 more new pairs open round the temporary pin R (N8). With the pair from pin 3, the pair from the first pin x and the 2 new pairs work a windmill crossing into pin J (N9). Remove temporary pin R and ease the pairs down round pin J. Pin the 2 right-hand pairs to the back of the pillow (N10). With the 2 left-hand pairs make a plait to pin K. Work a windmill crossing into pin K with these 2 pairs and the pairs from the second and third pins x. Leave the 2 right-hand pairs and with the 2 left-hand pairs make a plait to pin L.

Work a windmill crossing into pin L with these 2 pairs and the pairs from the fourth and fifth pins x. Leave the 2 right-hand pairs and make a plait with the 2 left-hand pairs from pin L to pin M. Work a windmill crossing into pin M with these 2 pairs and the last 2 pairs from the sixth and seventh pins x. Leave the 2 right-hand pairs and make the plait from pin M to pin N with the 2 left-hand pairs. Leave the 2 plait pairs ready to work pin N.

Push the pins down into the pillow out of the way and make the leaves into the centre pin-hole from pins J, K, L and M. Work the centre 8-pair crossing (N12) and make the leaves to pins N, P, Q and R. Work the windmill crossings into pins N, P, Q and R as the plait is made from pin N to pin R. Make the last plait from pin R to pin J and fasten off the 2 plait pairs into pin J using the needle technique explained on p. 10.

The pairs left at pins N, P, Q and R are used singly again and are twisted seven times each. These pairs are taken one after the other into the trail at the pin-holes marked ⊙ beginning at pin 10 (numbering here is for convenience). In turn, threads should be removed from the trail to accommodate these pairs as they are taken into it (N15).

Finishing

After taking in the last pair from pin R and removing 2 threads, take the weaver pair to pin T (Fig 34). Work the trail and ninepin at pin T – bring the new weaver pair to pin 1 where it fastens off. The trail passive pairs fasten off into the loops left on the pin when the lace was set up.

Work the ninepin from pin T to pin A and fasten off the 2 plait pairs into pin A. Make the plait from pin S to pin B and fasten these 2 pairs into pin B.

Cut off the bobbins – leaving long ends – remove the pins and weave the thread ends into the lace with a fine needle. If this piece is to be mounted then the ends from the plait threads can be taken through to the reverse side of the backing material. Follow instructions for finishing techniques on p. 11.

PATTERN 6   A CIRCULAR BORDER

Can be used as an edging for a mat, a pincushion, a lavender bag or as a frame round a family photograph.

12 pairs of bobbins wound in DMC Brillante d'Alsace 30.

An exercise in setting in and working the footside with whole stitch passive pairs.

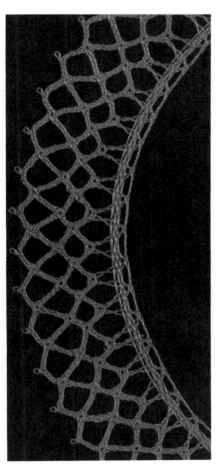

Pattern 6

Working notes (see Part III)

Footside. Weaver pair, edge pair and 2 pairs of passives, worked in whole stitch.

N6: Setting in 2 pairs at one pin.

N7: Hanging pairs in order.

N13b.i: Setting in 2 new pairs into one pin-hole, on the left.

N13b.ii: Taking in 2 plait pairs on the left, leaving immediately on same side.

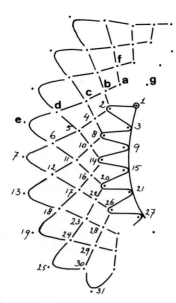

Figure 35
Pattern 6. Guide to pin-holes.

Figure 36
Setting in 2 pairs at pin 1.

Headside and Ground. Four sets of plaited pairs working in and out of the footside.
N8: Hanging pairs open.
N9b: Setting in 2 new pairs into a plait.
N2: Picots on the left of plait.
N9a: Windmill crossings.

Setting in the footside

Set in 2 pairs on pin 1. Follow Note 6 and refer to Figs 35 and 36. Twist the right-hand pair 3 times – this remains on the right-hand side as the edge pair. Twist the left-hand pair once – this is the weaver pair.

Hang 2 pairs of passives in order from the right (N7) on temporary pin *a*, above pin 1 (Fig 37).

Working the footside

This includes taking in 2 pairs at one pin-hole (N13b.ii). Work the weaver pair from pin 1 in whole stitch through both pairs of passives – twist the weaver pair once. Follow Fig 38.

●†Set in 2 new pairs at pin 2 to begin the plaits. Hang the 2 new pairs open round a temporary pin at *b* (N8). Take the weaver pair in whole stitch through both pairs – leave the weaver pair to the left of pin 2. Put up pin 2 between the two new pairs.†

Take the left-hand new pair in whole stitch through the right-hand new pair to enclose pin 2. Twist it once and take it as the new weaver pair in the footside to pin 3. Work it through the 2 passive pairs in whole stitch and twist it once – put up pin 3 to the left of the weaver pair, i.e. between the weaver pair and the last pair of passives worked through.

Remove temporary pin *b* and ease the new pairs down round pin 2. The left-hand new pair is now the weaver pair on the right of pin 3 so it will need a gentle easing across the passive pairs. The 'old' weaver pair and right-hand new pair are left out at pin 2 to make the plait.●

Edge pin

★The weaver pair is on the right-hand side of pin 3 (see Fig 38). Work a whole stitch with the weaver pair and the edge pair. Twist the right-hand pair 3 times; this is the new edge pair and it remains on the right-hand side of pin 3. Twist the left-hand pair once – this is the new weaver pair. The edge pin is to the *left* of *both* pairs. Do not enclose the edge pin with these 2 pairs. Bring the weaver pair in front of pin 3 and work it in whole stitch through the two passive pairs. Twist the weaver pair once. This movement encloses the edge pin.★

Leave the footside weaver pair ready to work pin 8 with the 2 pairs from the plait which are taken up at this pin.

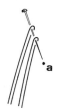

Figure 37
Passive pairs hung in order.

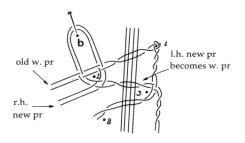

Figure 38
Setting in 2 new pairs at one pin-hole of
the footside.

Setting in the plait pairs for the headside and ground

Use Notes 9a-b for windmill crossings to set in 2 new pairs into a plait. The 'old' weaver pair from pin *1* and the new right-hand pair from pin *b* were left at pin *2* (Fig 35). Make a plait with these 2 pairs to pin *4*. At pin *4* two more new pairs are needed – hang these open (N8) round a temporary pin *c*. With these 2 pairs and the plait pairs from pin *2* work a windmill crossing into pin *4*. Leave the 2 right-hand pairs on the temporary pin *c* and with the 2 left-hand pairs make a plait from pin *4* to pin *5*.

Hang 2 more new pairs open round a temporary pin at *d*. With these 2 new pairs and the plait pairs from pin *4* work a windmill crossing into pin *5*. Leave the 2 right-hand pairs on the temporary pin and make a plait from pin *5* to pin *6* with the 2 left-hand pairs.

Hang 2 more new pairs open round a temporary pin at *e* and work a windmill crossing into pin *6* with these 2 pairs and the plait pairs from pin *5*. Leave the 2 right-hand pairs on the temporary pin. Use the 2 left-hand pairs from pin *6* to make the plait to pin *12*, working a left-hand single picot into pin *7*. Leave these 2 pairs ready to work pin *12*.

Remove the temporary pins *c*, *d* and *e* and ease the pairs down round pins *4*, *5* and *6*. With the 2 pairs from pin *4* make the plait to pin *8* in the footside.

Taking the plait pairs into the footside, Note 13b.ii

★★The weaver pair has worked through the passive pairs from pin *3* and has been twisted once. Now work it in whole stitch through the 2 pairs of the plait. Leave the weaver pair to the left of pin *8*. Put up pin *8* between the 2 plait pairs. The left-hand plait pair becomes the new weaver pair to pin *9*. Take it in whole stitch through the right-hand plait pair to enclose pin *8* – twist it once – then work it in whole stitch through the 2 passive pairs. Twist it once and work edge pin *9* following directions ★ to ★, above. The 'old' weaver pair and the 'old' right-hand plait pair remain out at pin *8* to make the next plait (to pin *10*).★★

Work the left-hand pair from pin *9* as the weaver pair through the 2 passive pairs – twist it once and leave it ready to work pin *14*. This encloses pin *9*.

Lift the temporary pin *a* keeping the passive pair loops on it and lay it behind pins *1* and *2*.

Working the plaits

★★★Return to pins *5* and *6* and make the plaits to pins *10* and *11*. Make the plait from pin *8* to pin *10*. Work a windmill crossing into pin *10*. Leave the 2 right-hand pairs and make the plait with the 2 left-hand pairs to pin *11*. Work a windmill crossing into pin *11* with these 2 pairs and the 2 pairs from pin *6*. Leave the 2 right-hand pairs – make a plait to pin *12* with the 2 left-hand pairs. Work a windmill crossing into pin *12* with these 2 pairs and the 2 pairs ready from pin *7*. Leave the 2 right-hand pairs and make the plait from pin *12* to pin *18*, working a left-hand single picot into pin *13*. Leave these 2 pairs ready at pin *18*. Make the plaits from pins *12* and *11* to pins *17* and *16* and leave the pairs ready to work these 2 pins. Make the plait from pin *10* to pin *14*.★★★

Take the plait pairs into the footside at pin *14* following instructions ★★ to ★★, above. Work the edge pin *15* and bring the weaver pair to pin *20*. Leave the weaver pair ready to work pin *20* after twisting it once. Work the plaits and windmill crossings from pin *14* setting pins *16, 17, 18* and picot *19*, and leaving pairs ready to work pins *24, 23, 22* and *20*. For this follow instructions ★★★ to ★★★.

Finishing

Work edge pin *g* and bring the weaver pair to pin *a*. Make the plait from pin *f* to pin *a*. Take in the plait pairs at pin *a*. Take the 'old' left-hand plait pair as the weaver pair to pin *1* and fasten it off here with the edge pair, following directions for the needle technique given on p. 10. Fasten the passive pairs into the loops. Finish making the plaits down the line *a* to *d*, working the windmill crossings into pins *b, c* and *d*. Leave the 2 left-hand pairs at pin *d*. Make the plaits to pins *2, 4* and *5*. Fasten the plait pairs into the lace at these pins using the needle technique, p. 10 and knot the pairs once only. Make the plait from pin *d* to pin *6* working the picot into pin *e*. Fasten these 2 pairs carefully into pin *6* as the picot can easily be spoilt. Knot the pairs once. Cut off the bobbins, remove the pins and lift the lace.

There are only plaits to weave the ends into. Follow instructions on p. 10 and weave them in carefully with a fine needle.

The footside passive pair threads, the weaver pair, the edge pair threads and the threads fastened into pin *2* can be woven into the footside passive pair trail.

PATTERN 7   ANOTHER CIRCULAR BORDER

Can be used the same way as Pattern 6

8 pairs of bobbins wound in DMC Brillante d'Alsace 30.

It is an exercise in setting in and working the footside with twisted passive pairs. It also reviews some of the techniques learnt so far.

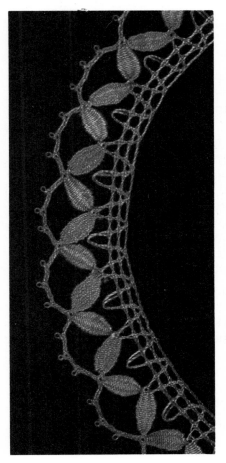

Pattern 7

Working notes (see Part III)

Footside. Worked with weaver pair and edge pair, and 2 pairs of passives working whole stitch and twist.

N6: Setting in 2 pairs on a pin.

N7: Hanging pairs in order on a temporary pin.

N13b.ii: Taking pairs into footside.

N13b.i: Setting in 2 new pairs at one pin-hole.

   Headside. Worked with 2 pairs for the leaves, 2 pairs for the plaits.

N9a-b: Windmill crossings.

N2: Single picots to the left of the plait.

N4: Leaves.

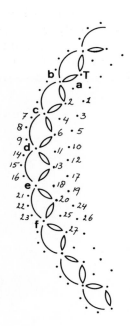

Figure 39
Pattern 7. Guide to pin-holes.

Setting in the footside

Set in 2 pairs on pin *1* (N6), (Fig 39). Twist the right-hand pair 3 times, the left-hand pair once. The right-hand pair remains to the right to become the edge pair, the left-hand pair is the weaver pair.

Hang the 2 pairs of passives in order from the right on the temporary pin *T* above pin *1*. The first pair of passives (on the right-hand side) will now be referred to as the outer pair. The second pair of passives (on the left) will be referred to as the inner pair.

Working the footside

Take the left-hand pair from pin *1*, the weaver pair, and work in whole stitch through the outer pair of passives – twist both pairs once. Work the weaver pair in whole stitch with the inner pair of passives – twist both pairs once.

Set in 2 new pairs at pin *2*. Follow instructions † to † in Pattern 6, and refer to Fig 40. The left-hand new pair becomes the weaver pair to pin *3*. Work it in whole stitch through the right-hand new pair – to enclose pin *2*. Twist it once. The 'old' weaver pair and right-hand new pair remain out at pin *2* to make the leaf to pin *c*. Remove temporary pin *b* and ease the new pairs down round pin *2*. Work the new weaver pair from pin *2* in whole stitch through the inner passive pair – twist both pairs once. Work the weaver pair in whole stitch with the outer passive pair – twist both pairs once. Put up the edge pin *3* to the left of the weaver pair. Set the edge pin as explained in Pattern 6, under ★ to ★.

★★Bring the weaver pair from pin *3* in whole stitch through the outer passive pair – twist both pairs once. Work the weaver pair in whole stitch with the inner passive pair – twist the passive pair once. At pin *4* no pairs enter or leave the footside. The weaver pair should be twisted 4 times round this pin; the pin is put up to the right of the weaver pair. With the weaver pair and each pair of passives in turn, work whole stitch – twist both pairs once; work back to pin *5*; twist both pairs once.★★

Make edge pin *5* and work to pin *6*. After working whole stitch with the inner pair of passives twist both pairs once and leave the weaver pair waiting to take in the 2 pairs from the leaf.

Lift the temporary pin *a*, keeping the loops on it, and lay it behind pins *1* and *2*.

Point to remember. At inner pin-holes of the footside at which no pairs enter or leave, twist the weaver pair 4 times, as in ★★ to ★★, above.

Headside

Return to pin *2* and make the leaf to pin *c*. Set in 2 new pairs at pin *c*, using a windmill crossing (N9a-b). Leave the 2 new pairs on the temporary pin and with the 2 left-hand pairs from pin *c* make the plait to pin *d*, working single left-hand picots into pins *7*, *8* and *9*. Leave the plait pairs ready at pin *d*. Remove the temporary pin and ease the 2 new pairs down into the lace at pin *c*. Make the leaf to pin *6* and take the 2 pairs into the footside following directions ★★ to ★★ in Pattern 6.

Continue the pattern, setting edge pin *10* and foot pin *11*, twisting the weaver pair 4 times at this pin, setting edge pin *12* and finally leaving the weaver pair ready to work pin *13*. Make the leaf from pin *6* to pin *d* and work a windmill crossing at pin *d*. From the windmill crossing, first make the plait to pin *e*, working single picots on the left-hand side, and then make the leaf to pin *13*. Continue the pattern.

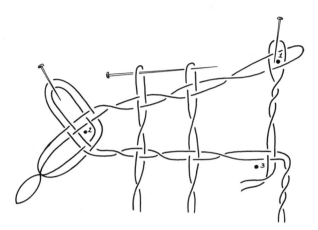

Figure 40
Setting in 2 new pairs at one pin-hole of twisted footside.

Finishing
The weaver pair from pin *a* and the edge pair fasten into pin *1* (see instructions on p. 8). The passive pairs fasten into the loops left on the pin. The 2 pairs from leaf *b* fasten into pin *2*. The 2 pairs from plait *b* to *c* fasten into pin *c*. Weave the thread ends carefully into the lace with a fine needle.

PATTERN 8 A HANDKERCHIEF OR MAT BORDER

15 pairs of bobbins wound in Bocken's linen 80, 2 extra pairs for the corner.

An exercise in connecting plait and leaf pairs into the inner part of the trail curve where, on the opposite side, the weaver pair must gain on a pin.

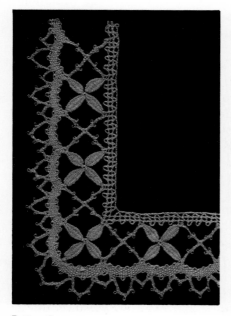

Pattern 8

Working notes (see Part III)

Trail. Worked with weaver pair and 4 passive pairs.

N7: Hanging pairs in order from a pin.

   Headside. Worked with 2 pairs making one plait.

N13b.i-ii: Setting in 2 new pairs.

   Ground. Worked with 4 pairs making plaits and leaves.

N17b.ii: Plaits and leaves taken into the trail while also gaining on a pin.

N9a: Windmill crossings in ground.

Footside. Worked with edge pair, weaver pair and 2 pairs of twisted passives.

N13b.ii: Working plait/leaf pairs into the footside.

    Corner. N11: Six-pair crossing.

N15: Removing threads.

Setting in the trail and headside

Hang the weaver pair on pin *1* and the 4 pairs of passives in order from the left on temporary pin *T*, above pin *1* (N7). See Fig 41. Take the weaver pair in whole stitch, through the passive pairs to pin *2*, twisting it once round pin *2*. Work to pin *3*; do not twist the weaver pair. Set in 2 new pairs at pin *3* (N13b.i). Leave out the 'old' weaver pair and the right-hand new pair for the plait at pin *3*. Using the left-hand new pair as the weaver pair set trail pin *4*, twisting the weaver pair once round the pin. Work to pin *5* – twist the weaver pair once – put up pin *5*; do not enclose it. Leave the weaver pair behind this pin. Lift the temporary pin *T*, keeping the passive loops on it and lay it behind pins *1* and *2*.

    At pin *5* the weaver pair has to gain on a pin (N17b.ii). At the same time 2 pairs have to be set in at pin *6* so as to leave out 2 pairs to work the plait in the ground. These 2 pins are opposite each other at the point on the trail curve.

Setting in 2 new pairs at pin 6 while gaining on pin 5

Hang the 2 new pairs open round a temporary pin above pin *6* (N8). Follow Fig 42. Work the left-hand new pair through the 4 pairs of passives in whole stitch and leave this pair on the left-hand side of the trail in front of pin *5*. Return to the right-hand side of the trail and put up pin *6* between the 2 right-hand trail passive pairs. These 2 pairs remain out of the trail at pin *6* to form the plait pairs. Bring the new right-hand pair from the temporary pin in whole stitch through these 2 passive pairs in front of pin *6*. This encloses pin *6*. Take this pair on through one more pair of passives into the trail. It now becomes the third passive pair in the trail from the left (see Fig 42):

    Counting from the left in the trail, the passive pairs at pins *5* and *6* now are:

        1. The new left-hand pair from the temporary pin.
        2. The original outer left-hand pair of the trail.
        3. The new right-hand pair from the temporary pin.
        4. The original second pair from the left of the trail.

    Return to pin *5* and enclose it by working the weaver pair across the trail passive pairs to pin *7*. Twist the weaver pair once and put up pin *7*. Remove temporary pin holding the 2 new pairs and ease these down into the trail. This method gives a neat flat appearance to the lace. To work at these points throughout the pattern follow Note 17b.ii: gaining on a pin while also taking in plait/leaf pairs.

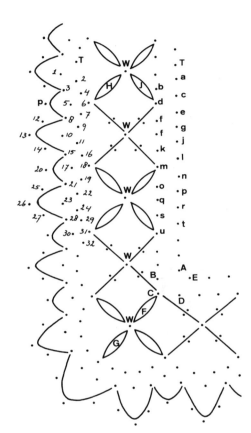

Figure 41
Pattern 8. Guide to pin-holes.

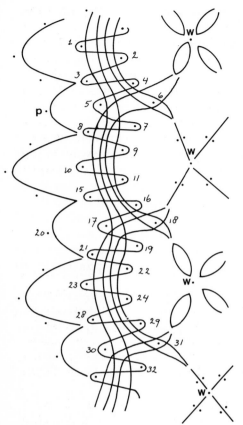

Figure 42
Working plait or leaf pairs into a point on the trail curve while also gaining on a pin on the opposite side.

Working the trail and headside

Refer to Figs 41 and 42. Return to pin *3* and make the plait to pin *8* working a single left-hand picot into pin *p*. Bring the weaver pair from pin *7* and take up the plait pairs at pin *8* following directions in Note 13b.ii. Leave out the 'old' weaver pair and the 'old' right-hand plait pair at pin *8*. Work the new weaver pair to pin *9* – twist once – put up pin *9* and work trail pins *10* and *11*. Work the weaver pair to pin *15*; do not twist it but leave it here ready for the plait pairs.

Return to pin *8* and make the plait to pin *15* working single, left-hand picots into pin-holes *12, 13* and *14*. With the weaver pair from pin *11* take up the plait pairs following instructions in Note 13b.ii. Bring the new trail weaver pair through the passive pairs and work trail pin *16*. Work the weaver pair back to pin *17* – twist it once – put up pin *17*. Do not enclose this pin but leave the weaver pair behind it. The trail weaver pair has to gain on this pin (equivalent to pin *5*). Follow Note 17b.ii.

Setting in the footside

Set in the weaver pair and the edge pair on pin *a* (N6) (Fig 41). Hang the 2 passive pairs in order on a temporary pin, above pin *a* (N7). Work the twisted footside as in Pattern 7 but at the inner pin-holes, beginning with *b*, at which no other pairs enter or leave, twist the weaver pair only once more for this pattern, making two twists on it at these pins.

Point to remember. Lift the temporary pin keeping the passive loops on it, and lay it behind pins *a* and *b*.

At pin *d* set in 2 new pairs following Note 13b.ii. Work the new weaver pair from pin *d* to pin *e* and continue the footside to pin *m*. Twist the weaver pair only once when the plait or leaf pairs are to be taken into the inner pin-holes as at pin *m*. Leave the weaver pair ready at pin *m*, to work later on with the plait pairs which will come across from pin *W*.

Working the ground

Make the 2 plaits, from pin *6* in the trail and *d* in the footside, working single picots on either side of both plaits. Work a windmill crossing into pin *W*. Make the plaits from pin *W* to pin *18* of the trail and pin *m* of the footside.

Working the footside

Take up the plait at pin *m* (N13b.ii) and work the twisted footside as in Pattern 7, giving the weaver pair 2 twists round the inner pin-holes at which no other pairs enter or leave. Continue the footside to pin-hole *u* and leave the weaver pair ready to work the inner pin *u*.

Working the plait pairs into the trail at pin *18*

Follow Note 17b.ii (gaining on a pin) and Figs 41 and 42. Bring the weaver pair in front of pin *17* and enclose this pin by taking it through the trail

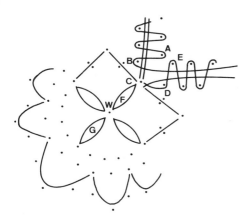

Figure 43
The corner.

passive pairs to pin-hole *19*. Twist it once and put up pin *19*. Leave the weaver pair here and return to pin *15*. Make the plait from pin *15* to pin *21* working the picot into pin *20*. Bring the trail weaver pair from pin *19* and take in the plait pairs at pin *21*. Work trail pins *22, 23* and *24* with the new weaver pair from pin *21* and leave the weaver pair ready to work pin *28*. Make the plait from pin *21* to pin *28* working the picots into pins *25, 26* and *27*. Take up the plait at pin *28* and bring the new weaver pair to pins *29* and *30*. Leave the weaver pair behind pin *30* after putting up the pin. This is equivalent to pins *5* and *17* and the trail gains on pin *30* again (N17b.ii).

Make the leaves from pin *18* of the trail and pin *m* of the footside. Work a windmill crossing into pin *W* and make the 2 leaves to pins *31* of the trail and *u* of the footside.

Continue the pattern into the corner.

The corner

Follow Fig 43. Take the weaver pair from pin *A* to pin *B* – set pin *B* in the usual manner – bring the weaver pair back through the 2 pairs of passives and leave it. It will become a footside passive pair. Two new pairs are set in at pin *C*. Hang these open round a temporary pin nearby (N8). Use the 2 new pairs, the 2 plait pairs ready at pin *C*, and the 2 footside passive pairs to work a six pair crossing (N11) into pin *C*. After working the six pair crossing remove the temporary pin and ease the new pairs down round pin *C*.

From the crossing at pin *C* the 2 left-hand pairs make leaf *F*; the 2 centre pairs work the plait; the 2 right-hand pairs return to the footside. With the 2 right-hand pairs work a whole stitch and twist both pairs once each. The right-hand pair of these 2 becomes a passive pair in the footside along with the old weaver pair. The left-hand pair becomes the new weaver pair for the footside. Put up pin *D* to the right of this pair. Bring the pair round from the left in front of pin *D* and work it in whole stitch and twist through the 2 passive pairs to pin *E*. Continue to make the footside in the usual manner.

After working leaf *G* in the corner the 2 pairs are taken into the trail. These are extra pairs and will not be needed until the next corner. Remove 2 pairs from the trail to accommodate them (N15).

Continue the pattern.

Finishing

The weaver pair and the edge pair in the footside fasten off into pin *a* (Fig 41); the footside passive pairs into the loops left on the pin. The pairs from leaf *J* fasten off into foot pin *d*. The trail weaver pair fastens into pin *1* and the passive pairs into the loops left on the pin. The pairs from the last plait to be made fasten into pin *3* and from the last leaf *H* into pin *6*.

PATTERN 9 AN OVAL MEDALLION MOTIF

Can be mounted in an oval frame or paper-weight
25 pairs, wound in DMC Brillante d'Alsace 50.

An exercise in exchanging the roles of passive and plait pairs at the point on the curve of a trail; setting in and working pairs on the right of a trail which leave immediately on the same side; taking plait pairs into a trail – not leaving immediately – and removing pairs from a trail.

Working notes (see Part III)

Trail. The trail is split with 3 passive pairs either side of a twisted weaver pair. Connect the plait from the scallop to the trail by following Note 13b.ii.

Headside scallop. This is worked with an edge pair, a weaver pair and 2 passive pairs. Two pairs work the plaits connecting the scalloped headside to the trail (connect these to the scallop, following Note 17c).

Centre design. This requires 12 pairs. They are set in, 2 each, at the pins marked ⊙, Nos 3, 11 and 21 and letters *a*, *b*, *c*. Follow Note 13b.iii to set in these pairs, and Note 13b.iv when connecting pairs to the right-hand side of the trail which leave immediately. Follow Note 14 to connect pairs which do not immediately leave the trail and Note 15 for removing threads.

Other notes to follow are:
N6: Setting in 2 pairs at one pin.
N7: Hanging pairs in order.
N8: Hanging pairs open.
N3: Picots.
N9a: Windmill crossing.
N13b.i: Setting in 2 new pairs on the left.
Instructions for finishing the lace, p. 8.

Setting in the trail

Hang the weaver pair on pin *1* (see Fig 44). Hang six pairs in order from the right on a temporary pin, above pin *2* (N7). Take the weaver pair in whole stitch through the first three passive pairs – twist the weaver pair once – work in whole stitch through the next three passive pairs. Twist the weaver pair once and set pin *2*. Bring the weaver pair back through 3 passive pairs in whole stitch – twist it once and work whole stitch through the next *3* passive pairs. Do not twist the weaver pair.

Hang 2 pairs open on a temporary pin near pin-hole *3*. Take the weaver pair through the 2 new pairs (N13b.iii) and put up pin *3*. Work the new weaver pair in whole stitch through 3 passive pairs – twist it once – work whole stitch through the next 3 passive pairs – twist the weaver pair once and set pin *4*. Remove the temporary pin and ease the new pairs down. Leave out 2 pairs at pin *3* for the plait.

Pattern 9

Lift the temporary pin, holding the trail passive pairs and lay them back behind pins *1* and *2* keeping the loops on it.

Work trail pins *5*, *6* and *7* in the same way as pin *4*. Take the weaver pair from pin *7* to pin *8* and set in 2 new pairs on the left at pin *8* (N13b.i). Leave 2 pairs to make the plait and take the new weaver pair through the trail setting pins *9* and *10*. Work to pin *11*. Set in 2 new pairs on the right (N13b.iii) at pin *11*. Take the new weaver pair through the trail and set pins *12* and *13*, leaving 2 pairs at pin *11* to make the leaf (N4).

Important note. Work the centre design as the pairs are set in and become available for this, otherwise pins in the lace make it awkward to work the leaves. Make the plait from pin *3* and the leaf from pin *11* and anchor these temporarily with pins pushed right down into the pillow.

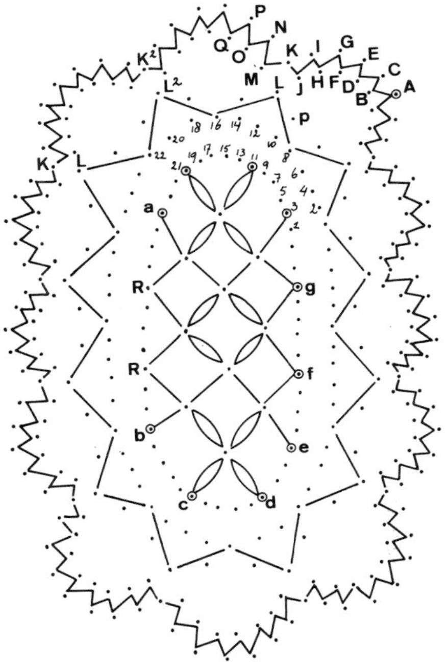

Setting in the scallop

Set in 2 pairs on a pin at *A* (N6). Twist both pairs twice. Hang 2 pairs in order on a pin above pin-hole *B*.

★Take the right-hand pair from pin *A* in whole stitch through the 2 passive pairs – twist it once and set pin *B*. Work back in whole stitch through the 2 passive pairs. Twist the weaver pair twice. Work a whole stitch with the weaver pair and the edge pair – twist both pairs once and set pin *C* between them. Enclose pin *C* with a whole stitch and twist both pairs twice.★

Take the right-hand pair from *C* as the weaver pair in whole stitch through the 2 passive pairs – twist it once and set pin *D*. Work back in whole stitch through the 2 passive pairs and twist the weaver pair twice. Work a whole stitch with the edge pair and twist both pairs once – set pin *E* between them. Enclose pin *E* with a whole stitch and twist both pairs twice. Lift the temporary pin, keeping the passive pair loops on it and lay it back behind pins *A* and *B*.

Continue the scallop following instructions ★ to ★, above, setting pins *F* to *K*. Leave the weaver pair and the edge pair at pin *K* after enclosing the pin with a whole stitch and twisting both pairs twice.

Working the plait into the scallop

Make the plait from pin *8*, working double picot *P* on the left (N3), until the plait just reaches pin *L*. Follow Note 17c to work the plait pairs into the scallop – to become passive pairs, and the passive pairs out from the scallop to become the plait pairs. In this case the weaver pair has been left at pin *K* where it gains on that pin at the point of the curve (N17c). Use the passive pairs at pin *L* to make the plait to pin *16*, with a double picot set to the left. Leave these 2 pairs ready at pin *16*.

Bring the right-hand pair from pin *K* as the weaver pair and work whole stitch through the new passive pairs – twist it once and set in pin *M*. Continue the scallop, setting pins *N*, *O*, *P*, *Q* as above, under ★ to ★. Finish the scallop at the equivalent of pins *K* and *L*, leaving the edge pair and the

Figure 44
Pattern 9. Guide to pin-holes.

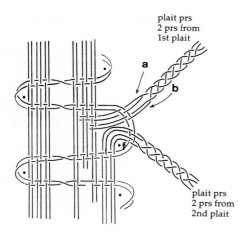

plait prs
2 prs from
1st plait

a

b

·f

plait prs
2 prs from
2nd plait

Figure 45
Finishing the lace at pins *f* & *g*.
a. Count as 4th pair, work through pairs
5 & 6 and then lay to back of pillow.

b. Count as 3rd pair, work through pair
4 and then lay to the back of the pillow.

weaver pair at pin *K2*. The passive pairs will become plait pairs at pin *L2* when the plait from pin *16* is made (N17c).

Return to the trail and set pins *14* and *15*, work to pin *16* taking in the plait on the left (N13b.ii). Take the new weaver pair through the trail and set pins *17, 18, 19* and *20*. Make the plait from pin *16* to pin *L2* and use Note 17c to change plait pairs into the scallop passive pairs and the scallop passive pairs into the next plait pairs.

Setting in and working the centre
Make the third scallop until the equivalent of pins *K* and *L*. Return to the trail and work to pin *21*, setting in 2 new pairs on the right (N13b.iii) at pin *21*. Make trail pin *22*, taking in the plait pairs from pin *L2* on the left (N13b.ii). Leave the trail and scallop and work the next part of the centre.

Make the leaf from pin *21*. Cross the leaves from pin *11* and pin *21* in a windmill crossing (N9a) and work the 2 leaves from the crossing. Anchor these temporarily. Continue the pattern, working the centre as the pattern progresses, setting in 2 new pairs on the right of the trail at each of pins *a* and *b* (N13b.iii). At pins *R* the plait from the centre connects to the trail on the right (Note 13b.iv). When pin *d* of the trail is reached the 2 pairs of the leaf are taken in (N14). These pairs are no longer needed, but should be kept on the right-hand side of the trail. Threads from the other 3 passive pairs of the right-hand side should be removed to accommodate them (N15). Remove 4 threads over the next 2 rows of the trail.

When pin *f* of the trail is reached 4 pairs of bobbins from 2 plaits need to be taken into the trail (see Fig 45). Work in the following manner (see also N14).

★★Take the weaver pair in whole stitch through the first 2 pairs (using 2 threads of the pair as one; Note 14) – and then through the second 2 pairs. Put in pin *f* between the weaver pair and the last pair worked through. Use all threads singly again. Leave the weaver pair behind pin *f*. Now, counting from the right-hand side – take the fourth pair from the right (a plait pair) in whole stitch through the fifth and sixth pairs of passives. Lay this pair to the back of the pillow. Count from the right again – take the third pair from the right (a plait pair) in whole stitch through the fourth pair. Now lay this pair to the back of the pillow. These movements take the first 2 plait pairs in whole stitch through the passive pairs and then they are laid to the back of the pillow. This anchors the plait pairs in the lace and removes the need to weave in threads when the work is finished. These pairs can be cut close to the lace later when some pins have been removed. Trim off the bobbins before removing the pins.

Now bring the weaver pair from behind pin *f* in front of it and work whole stitch through the five passive pairs – twist it once – work whole stitch through the three left-hand passive pairs of the trail – pin on the opposite side to pin *f*. Work the trail in the normal way, removing threads from the right-hand side (N15) to accommodate the 2 extra pairs of the second plait taken in at pin *f*.★★

Repeat this procedure ★★ to ★★ at pin *g* when 4 pairs are taken in again from 2 plaits.

Finishing

Fasten the trail passive pairs into the loops left on the pin. Fasten the weaver pair into pin *1*. The 2 pairs from the last plait made from the scallop to the trail fasten off into pin *8* of the trail.

Fasten the scallop passive pairs into the loops left on the pin. Fasten off the edge pair and the weaver pair of the scallop into pin *A*.

Weave thread ends into the whole stitch areas of the trail and the scallop, using a needle.

PATTERN 10 EDGING FOR A HANDKERCHIEF OR MAT

18 pairs, wound in Campbell's linen 100 or B.D.U.C. linen 100. 10 extra pairs will be needed for the corner.

An exercise in connecting plait pairs on the right:

    a. which do not leave immediately; removing pairs to accommodate them.

    b. on the curve while gaining on a trail pin.

Pattern 10

42

Working notes (see Part III)

Trail. Worked with weaver pair + 3 passive pairs.

N13b.ii: Connecting plait pairs on the left which leave immediately.

N13b.iii: Setting in 2 new pairs on the right of the trail.

N14: Connecting plait pairs on the right which do not leave immediately.

N15: Removing pairs to accommodate the latter.

N17b.ii: Connecting plait pairs on the right – on the curve while gaining on a trail pin.

    Footside. Weaver pair and edge pair, 2 passive pairs worked in whole stitch.

N13.ii: Plait pairs which connect and leave immediately.

    Headside. 4 pairs for the 2 plaits – one working in and out of the trail and the other working parallel to it.

    Ground. 6 pairs – 4 set in from the trail and 2 set in from the footside.

N1: Plaits.

N4: Leaves.

Windmill crossings (N9a) are worked in the ground and headside whenever 4 pairs meet.

Setting in the trail

Hang the weaver pair on pin *1* and the 3 passive pairs on a temporary pin in order from the right, above pin *2* (N7); see Fig 46. Work trail pins *2* and *3* and take the weaver pair to pin *A*. Set in 2 new pairs at pin *A* (N13.i) and take the new weaver pair to pin *4*. Lift the temporary pin, keeping the trail passive pair loops on it and lay it behind pins *1* and *2*. Work trail pins *4*, *5* and *6* and take the weaver pair to pin *7*. Twist it once – put up pin *7* and leave the weaver pair behind it.

Setting in the footside

Set in 2 pairs on pin *1* (N6), Fig 46. Twist the right-hand pair twice and the left-hand pair once. Hang 2 passive pairs on a temporary pin above pin *2*. Work the footside with whole stitch passive pairs as directed in Pattern 6, p. 28. At the inner pins of the footside at which no pairs enter or leave twist the weaver pair 3 times before setting the pin.

    At pin *4* set in 2 new pairs to begin the plait (N13b.ii). Work the footside taking in the plait or leaf pairs at appropriate pin-holes (N13b.ii) as in Pattern 6. Remember to twist the weaver pair only once at these pin-holes. After working edge pin *9* bring the weaver pair to pin *10* – twist it once and leave it ready to take in the plait pairs from pin *8* of the trail.

    Make the plait from pin *4* of the footside to pin *8* of the trail working a left-hand picot into pin *P* (N3).

Return to the trail

The weaver pair was left at pin *7*. Take in the plait pairs at pin *8* using Note 17b.ii, while gaining on trail pin *7*. After working in the plait pairs and

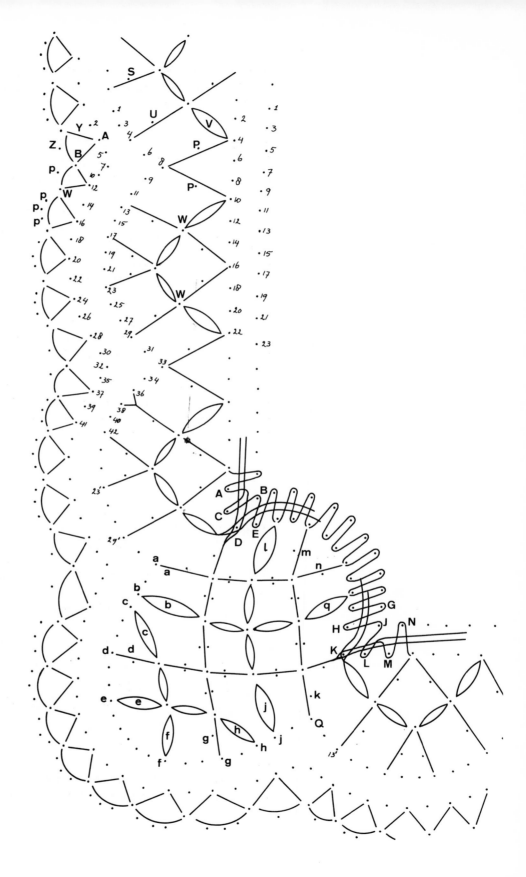

Figure 46
Pattern 10. Guide to pin-holes.

44

leaving 2 passive pairs out of the trail at pin *8*, take the weaver pair from pin *7* to pin *9*. Put up pin *9* and work trail pins *10* and *11*. Take the weaver pair to pin *12* – do not twist it – leave it ready at pin *12*.

Setting in and working the headside

Return to pin *A* and make the plait to pin *B*. Set in 2 new pairs at pin *B* (N9a-b). With the left-hand pairs make the plait to pin *W* working the picot into pin *p*. With the right-hand pairs make the plait to the trail and take these into the trail at pin *12* – leaving 2 pairs out to plait to pin *W*, working a windmill with the outer plait pairs. Take the new weaver pair to pin *13* and set in 2 new pairs (N13b.iii), leaving 2 pairs out to work the plait in the ground. This leaves the trail on the right at pin *13*.

Take the new right-hand pair as the weaver pair to pin *14* – set this pin and work pin *15*. At pin *16* take in the 2 pairs of the outer plait and at pin *17* set in 2 more new pairs as at pin *13*. Continue to work the trail, headside, ground and footside, taking in plait or leaf pairs at appropriate pin-holes until pin *23* of the trail. Take in the plait pairs at pin *23* (N14) and remove pairs to accommodate them (N15).

At pin *29* take in the 2 pairs of the plait (N14). Keep these 2 pairs in the trail and leave them out, one at each of 2 adjacent pin-holes, at pins *36* and *38* (N14). Pin *38* is the equivalent of pin *13*. Make the plait from pin *38* with these 2 pairs. At pin *42*, two new pairs must be set in again for the plait (N13b.iii). Work the pattern to the corner.

The corner

Footside

Take the weaver pair to pin *A* – put up pin *A* and take the weaver pair back through the 2 passive pairs – do not twist it. Leave the weaver pair here. Take the outer passive pair in whole stitch through the inner passive pair – twist it once and put up pin *C*. Retain this pair as the weaver pair – work through inner passive and old weaver pair – twist it once and put up pin *B*. Leave the weaver pair and the edge pair behind pin *B*. The work gains on pin *B* (N17). At pin *D* change the function of the footside passive pairs and the leaf pairs (N17c). Take the inner passive pair through the 2 pairs of the leaf – put up pin *D* between the leaf pairs – take the outer passive pair through the 2 pairs of the leaf. The 2 passive pairs are left out to make the plait and the 2 leaf pairs become the footside passive pairs. Make up the edge pin *B* and bring the weaver pair through the 2 new passive pairs to pin *E*. Set this pin in the normal way and continue the footside as usual, setting in 2 new pairs each for leaf *1* and plait *m* (N13b.i).

Headside

Two new pairs need to be set in at each of the pins *a*, *c*, *d* and *e*; 2 pairs should be left out of the trail at *b*, equivalent to pin *13*. At pin *a* follow Note

17b.ii, to set in the new pairs, as the trail must gain on the pin opposite at the same time. At pins *c*, *d* and *e* follow Note 13b.iii.

Centre of the corner

Work the plaits and leaves in the centre using windmill crossings (N9a) whenever 4 pairs meet; while also gradually working the footside to pin *G* and the headside to pin *Q* as the appropriate leaves and plaits have been made. After taking in the pairs from plait *n* and leaf *q* on the footside, pairs should be removed to accommodate them (N15). On the headside the pairs from the plait and leaves *f*, *g*, *h* and *j*, are taken in and pairs should be removed to accommodate them (N15).

Return to the footside

Take the weaver pair from pin *G* to pin *H* – twist it once – put up pin *H* and bring the weaver pair back through the 2 passive pairs. Twist the weaver pair once – put up pin *J* and leave the weaver pair behind it. Take the inner passive pair in whole stitch through the 2 pairs of the plait at pin *K*. Put up pin *K* between the plait pairs. Take the outer passive pair in whole stitch through the 2 pairs of the plait. The passive pairs are left out at pin *K* to make the leaf; the plait pairs become the footside passive pairs. Make up edge pin *J* and bring the weaver pair to pin *L* through the 2 new passive pairs. Put up pin *L* and take the weaver pair back through the 2 passive pairs; do not twist it but leave it here. Take the outer passive pair as the weaver pair to pin *M*. Retain this pair as the weaver pair and continue the footside in the normal way, leaving the weaver pair from pin *L* as the new outer passive pair.

Return to the headside

Take up the pairs from plait *k* into the trail at pin *Q*. These plait pairs do not immediately leave the trail but the trail *does* have to gain on a pin at this point. An adaptation of Note 17a is therefore necessary. Incorporate it with Note 14 to take in the plait pairs. Retain the plait pairs in the trail and leave out 2 pairs at the next plait – equivalent to pin *13*: shown on Fig 46 as *13'*.

This completes the corner. Continue the pattern.

Finishing

Footside. The weaver pair and edge pair fasten into pin *1* – the passive pairs into the loops left on the pin. The last leaf *V* fastens off into pin *4*.

Trail. The weaver pair fastens into pin *1*, the passive pairs into the loops left on the pin. After taking plait *S* into the trail remove 4 threads to accommodate these pairs so that there will be only the original number of passive pairs. The pairs from plait *U* fasten into pin *4* and the pairs from plait *Y* into pin *A*. The pairs from plait *Z* fasten into pin *B*.

PATTERN 11   A CIRCULAR BORDER

22 pairs wound in Bocken's linen 80.

An exercise in taking leaf pairs through a trail; joining trail and footside by a 'kiss'; half-stitch circles in ground and headside worked with plait and leaf pairs.

Note. this pattern is designed to show the movement of plait pairs through the trail so the guide lines should be drawn in exactly as shown on the pricking.

Pattern 11

Working notes (see Part III)

Trail. Worked with 5 passive pairs and a weaver pair.

N16: Taking leaf pairs 'through' the trail (entering on one side and leaving on the opposite side).

N14: Plait pairs not leaving trail immediately.

N13b.iii: Setting in new pairs on the right, leaving immediately.

Half-stitch circles in the ground and headside. These are worked from the plait and leaf pairs.

Footside. The footside is worked with 2 passive pairs and can be made twisted, as shown on Plate 11, or with whole stitch passive pairs.

N13b.ii: Working plait pairs on the left, leaving immediately.

N18: Kiss – joins the trail to the footside at points marked *x* (Fig 47).

Setting in the trail

Hang the weaver pair on pin *1* and the trail passive pairs in order from the left (N7), on a temporary pin *x*, above pin *2* (Fig 47). Set trail pins *2* and *3*, and work to pin *4*. Lift the temporary pin, keeping the passive pair loops on it and lay it behind pins *1* and *2*.

Set in 2 new pairs at pin *4* as explained in Note 13b.iii, leaving out the 'old' weaver pair and the new left-hand pair to make the plait to the footside. Bring the new right-hand pair to pin *5* as the weaver pair. Work to trail pins *5*, *6* and *7* and bring the weaver pair to pin *8*. Set in 2 new pairs at pin *8* as at pin *4*. Leave out the 'old' weaver pair and the new left-hand pair to make the plait from pin *8*. Work trail pins *9*, *10* and *11*, and at pin

Figure 47
Pattern 11. Guide to pin-holes.

12 set in 2 new pairs as at pin *4*. Bring the new right-hand pair as the weaver pair and work to pin *13*. Set trail pins *13* and *14* and bring the weaver pair to pin *A*. Set in 2 new pairs for the ninepin at pin *A* by following Note 13b.i, leaving out the 'old' weaver pair and the new right-hand pair to begin the ninepin. Use the new left-hand pair as the weaver pair and work trail pins *15, 16* and *17* – twist the weaver pair once – put up pin *17* and leave the weaver pair here behind it.

Setting in the ninepin

Make the plait from pin *A* to pin *B*. Set in 2 new pairs at pin *B* using a windmill crossing (N9a-b). Leave the 2 right-hand pairs on the temporary pin and make the plait from *B* to *C* with the 2 left-hand pairs. Set in 2 more pairs at pin *C* as at pin *B*. Leave the 2 right-hand pairs on the temporary pin and with the 2 left-hand pairs from pin *C* make the plait to pin *F*, working 4 picots set to the left. Leave these 2 pairs ready at pin *F*. Remove the temporary pins and ease the pairs down at pins *B* and *C*. Make the plaits from *B* to *D* and *C* to *D* and work a windmill crossing at pin *D*. Take the 2 left-hand pairs in a plait from pin *D* to pin *F* and work the windmill crossing into pin *F*. Make the plaits from pin *F* to *H* and *F* to *G*. Leave the pairs ready at pins *H* and *G*.

Return to the trail

★With the 2 pairs remaining at pin *D* make a plait to pin *E* of the trail. Put up pin *E* between the 2 plait pairs. Take the right-hand plait pair across the trail to pin *17* – twist it once and leave it in front of pin *17*. This pair and the 'old' weaver pair make the plait from pin *17* to pin *b*. Use the left-hand plait pair as the new weaver pair in the trail (Refer to Note 16a). Take it through the passive pairs to pin *18* – twist it once – put up pin *18* and work to pin *G*.★

Take in the plait pairs at pin *G* (N13b.ii). Make trail pins *19* and *20* – work to pin *21* – twist the weaver pair once – put up pin *21* and work to pin *K*. Leave the weaver pair at pin *K*.

★★After enclosing pin *21* and taking the weaver pair back across the trail, 2 pairs are left out to make the plait *M*. This reduces to 3 the number of passive pairs in the trail between pins *21* and *28*. The 2 pairs return to the trail from plait *N*, making 5 pairs again. Each time this point at the top of the trail is reached (equivalent to pin *21*), leave out 2 passive pairs to make the plait to the inner circle. They return to the trail from the circle in plait *N*; follow Note 14 to take in these pairs.★★

Return to the ninepin

Work the ninepin from pin *G* to pin *K* taking the plait pairs into the trail at pin *K*. Work trail pins *22* to *26*. Make the ninepin and take in the plait pairs at pin *27*. Leave the trail and the ninepin at pin *28*.

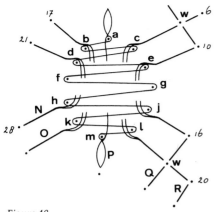

Figure 48
Half-stitch circle.

Working the ground

With the pairs left out of the trail at pins *4, 8, 17* and *21* make the plaits, and with the 2 pairs from pin *12* make the leaf. Anchor these pairs temporarily until they are needed.

Setting in the footside

Set in the edge pair and the weaver pair on pin *1*. For whole stitch passive pairs follow instructions in Pattern 6 and twist the weaver pair 4 times round inner pins at which no pairs enter or leave.

For twisted passive pairs follow Pattern 7 and twist the weaver pair 3 times at inner pins at which no pairs enter or leave.

At pin-holes where plait pairs are taken in, twist the weaver pair only once. The plait from pin *4* of the trail is taken into the footside at pin *6* (follow Note 13b.ii).

Return to the ground

Make the plait from pin *6* of the footside and work a windmill crossing (N9a) into pin *w* with the plait from pin *8* of the trail. Make the plait with the 2 left-hand pairs to enter the circle at pin *c*. Make the plait with the 2 right-hand pairs to the footside and take it in at pin *10*. After setting edge pin *11* make the plait from pin *10* to circle pin *e*.

Setting in the half-stitch circle

Follow Note 19c.i and Fig 48. Put up pin *a* between the 2 pairs of the leaf, enclose in half-stitch and use the left-hand pair as the weaver pair. Remember to work through the plait pairs singly in half-stitch when taking them into the pin-holes but take in 2 pairs at each of the pin-holes *b*, *c*, *d* and *e*. Work and enclose pins *f* and *g* with the weaver pair without taking in or leaving out pairs. Leave 2 pairs out at pins *h*, *j*, *k* and *l* after enclosing the pins and working back across the circle.

Set pin *m* with the last 2 pairs and enclose it with a whole stitch ready to make the leaf *P*. Make this leaf and the plaits *N* and *O*. Leave these ready to be taken into the trail. Make the plait from pin *j* and take this into the footside at pin *16*. After setting edge pin *17* make the plait from pin *16* and work the windmill crossing at pin *w* with the plait from pin *1* of the circle. Make the left-hand plait *Q* from pin *w* and leave this ready to enter the trail. Work the right-hand plait and take it into foot pin *20*; set edge pin *21*. Make plait *R* from pin *20* and leave it ready to enter the trail.

Return to the trail

At pin *28* take in the pairs from plait *N* as if they were only one pair and when enclosing the pin work them singly (N14). The trail now has 5 passive pairs again. Work the trail and ninepin until pin *33*. From this pin until pin *49* the plait and leaf pairs from the inner half-stitch circle and the ground work through the trail and make: plait *O* in the ninepin, which

51

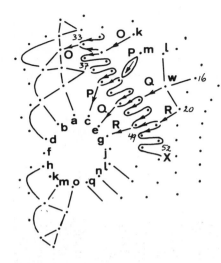

Figure 49
Working plait pairs 'through' the trail to the left.

eventually works into the outer circle; plaits *P, Q* and *R* which also work the outer circle (see Fig 49). Follow Note 16b to work the plait pairs through the trail to the left.

Remember to twist the weaver pair once when leaving it behind the pin and twist the left-hand plait pair once when leaving it in front of the pin. Take in the ninepin plait pairs as usual, at pin *37*.

Work the trail weaver pair on to pin *52* and leave it behind this pin after twisting it. Finish working the ninepin to the circle and make the plaits *P, Q* and *R* from pins *39, 43* and *47*, ready to make the outer half-stitch circle (Fig 47).

Outer half-stitch circle

Work this in the same way as the inner one, this time putting up pin *a* between the 2 plait pairs (see Fig 49). Take the left-hand pair as the weaver pair to pin *b*. Bring in 2 pairs at the pins *b, c, d, e* and *g*. Pins *f, j* and *k* are made up with the weaver pair without pairs entering or leaving. After each enclosing of pins *h, l, m, n, o* and *q*, 2 pairs are left out. Make the plaits from the circle to the trail.

Return to the trail and footside

The weaver pair was left at pin *52*. Work the footside down to pin *26*.

The weaver pairs from the footside and the trail work a kiss between pins *52* of the trail and *26* of the footside (N18); Fig 50. Take the left-hand pair from the kiss as the weaver pair in the trail and the right-hand pair into the footside. Set edge pin *27*.

Work the trail from pin *52* to pin *62* (Fig 50), at the same time bringing the plait pairs from the outer circle through to work the inner circle again. Follow Note 16a to work plait pairs through to the right. Take the left-hand pair of the plait from pin *61* as the weaver pair to pin *62*. Work the trail and ninepin taking the plait pairs in at pin *A* again (see Fig 50). The plait pairs *O* are left out of the trail at pin *17* again (Fig 47) using the pairs from pin *E*, see ★ to ★, above.

The plait pairs *M* are left out of the trail from the passive pairs, see ★★ to ★★ above. Continue the pattern.

Finishing

The footside weaver pair and edge pair fasten into pin *1*. The passive pairs of the trail and the footside fasten into their respective loops left on the pins.

The trail weaver pair fastens into pin *1* of the trail. After making up the last outer circle the plait pairs fasten into the trail pins *5* and *9*, and the leaf pairs into pin *13*.

The ninepin fastens off into pin *A* of the trail and into pins *B* and *C* of the ninepin.

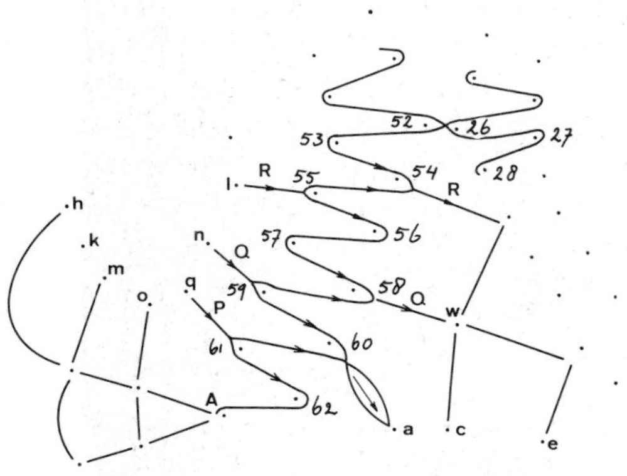

Figure 50
Working the 'kiss' and bringing plait pairs 'through' the trail to the right.

PATTERN 12   AN OVAL MAT

37 pairs wound in Bocken's linen 80.

An exercise in crossing trails. One plait running on the outer edge with picots *P* set to the left. Draw in the guidelines on the pricking in exactly the position marked.

Working notes (see Part III)

N20b: Crossing trails on the outside. Leaves in the centre of the crossing trails are worked in the directions indicated by the arrows.

N14: Pairs entering the left-hand side trail, remaining in it for several pin-holes.

Pattern 12

N16a: Leaf pairs working through the right-hand side trails (Fig 52) to form plait pairs in the ground – the latter returning through the trail of the next repeat (N16b) to form the leaves in its centre (Fig 53).

N9: Windmill crossings.

N11: Six pair crossing.

The centre trail is divided by twisting the weaver pair between 2 pairs of passives each side.

N13b.ii: Leaf pairs from the ground connecting to the centre trail on the left.

N13b.iii: Setting in new pairs on the right.

Setting in the outer trails

Left-hand trail. Hang the weaver pair on pin *1*, and 5 passive pairs in order (N7) on a temporary pin above pin *1*, Fig 51. Set trail pin *2* and work to pin *3*; do not twist the weaver pair but leave it at pin *3*.

Right-hand trail. Hang the weaver pair on pin *1*, and 5 pairs of passives in order from the left on a temporary pin; set trail pin *2*. Work to pin *3* – do not twist the weaver pair.

Lift the temporary pins on each side keeping passive pair loops on them and lay them behind pins *1* and *2* on each side.

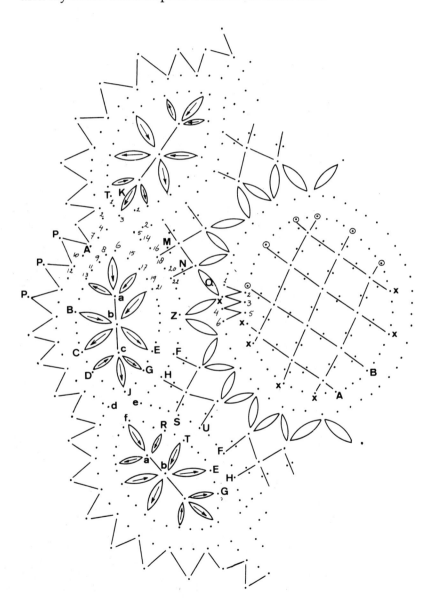

Figure 51
Pattern 12. Guide to pin-holes.

Crossing the trails at pins *3, 4, 5* and *6*

Follow Fig 51. Work a whole stitch with the weaver pairs. Put up pin *3* between them – enclose the pin with whole stitch. Take the left-hand pair to pin *4* through the left-hand passive pairs. Take the right-hand pair to pin *5* through the right-hand passive pairs. Twist the weaver pairs once each – put up pins *4* and *5* and leave the weaver pairs behind these pins.

Work the passive pairs through each other in whole stitch. This crosses them over. Bring the weaver pairs from pins *4* and *5* through their 'new' passive pairs to pin *6*. Work a whole stitch with the weaver pairs – put up pin *6* between them – enclose pin *6* with a whole stitch. Leave these 2 pairs at pin *6* to make the leaf. Use the inner passive pairs lying on the right and left of pin *6* as the weaver pairs to work the trail to pins *14* and *7* respectively. These 2 pairs remain as the trail weaver pairs for each side until the next crossing (N20b). The trails now work separately. There are now only 4 passive pairs in each trail; continue with only 4 passive pairs.

Working the trails

The left-hand trail

Set pins *7* and *8* in the left-hand side trail and work to pin *A* – set in 2 new pairs at pin *A* (N13b.i). Bring the new weaver pair across the trail to pin *9* and set the pin. Make the plait from *A* with picot at *P* and then on to *12*. Set trail pins *10, 11* and *12* taking in the plait pairs at pin *12* (N13b.ii). Take the new weaver pair from pin *12* to pin *13* and leave it ready to work here.

The right-hand trail

Return to pin *6* and take the inner passive pair as weavers to pin *14*.

Set trail pins *15* and *16* and work to pin *17*. Set in 2 new pairs at pin *17* (N13b.i) and with the new weaver pair from pin *17* set trail pins *18, 19* and *20* – work to pin *21*. Set in 2 new pairs at pin *21* as at pin *17*. Work the new weaver pair to pin *22* and leave it, and the trail, here.

Working the leaves and the left-hand trail

Make the leaf from pin *6* and the leaf from pin *17*. Work the windmill crossing at pin *a*. Take the 2 right-hand pairs in a plait to pin *b* and make the leaf to pin *13* with the 2 left-hand pairs. Take these 2 pairs into the trail (N14). They remain in the trail until pin *B*. Work the trail and outer plait with picots until pin *B* is reached. Put up pin *B* and work back across the trail – leave out the 2 pairs after enclosing pin *B*. Work the trail and outer plait until pin *C* is reached. Leave the trail weaver pair here.

Make the leaves from pin *B* and pin *21*. Work a six-pair crossing at pin *b* (N11). With the 2 right-hand pairs make the leaf to pin *E* on the right-hand trail. Anchor this leaf into pin *E* temporarily. With the 2 centre pairs make the plait to pin *c*. With the 2 left-hand pairs make the leaf to pin *C* on the left-hand trail. Take these 2 leaf pairs into the trail (N14). They remain in the trail until pin *D* is reached. Work the left-hand trail and the outer plait as far as pin *D* – put up pin *D* and take the weaver pair across the trail to the left. Leave out the 2 pairs after enclosing pin *D*. Work the left-hand trail and outer plait as far as pin *J* and leave the weaver pair and the trail here. Make the leaf from pin *D* to pin *c* – work a windmill crossing into pin *c*. Make the 2 leaves to pins *G* and *J* and anchor them temporarily in these pin-holes.

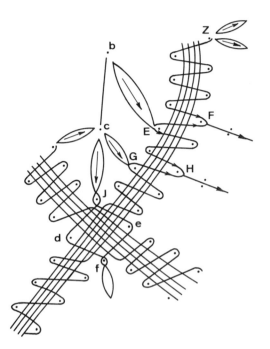

Figure 52
Taking leaf pairs through the trail, to the right.

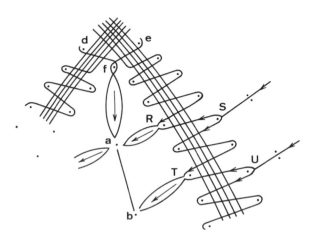

Figure 53
Taking plait pairs through the trail, to the left.

Setting in the centre trail and plaited centre

Hang the weaver pair on pin *1*, and 4 pairs of passives in order from the left on a temporary pin above pin *1*, marked ⊙ on Fig 51. Take the weaver pair in whole stitch through the first 2 passive pairs – twist the weaver pair once and work through the second 2 passive pairs. Twist the weaver pair once and put up pin *2*. Work to pin *X* through 2 pairs in whole stitch – twist the weaver pair once – work through the remaining 2 pairs in whole stitch. At pin *X* set in 2 new pairs (N13b.i). Take the left-hand new pair as the weaver pair through 2 passive pairs – twist it once and work through the second 2 passive pairs. Twist the weaver pair once and put up pin *3*. Lift the temporary pin holding the passive pairs and lay it behind pins *1* and *2*. Continue to work the inner trail with one twist on the weaver pair between the 2 passive pairs on each side. Set the pins *4*, *5* and *6*.

57

At each of the pins marked x on the inner side of the centre trail 2 new pairs are set in to work the plaited centre (N13b.iii). At pin A in the centre trail the 2 pairs from the first pin x work out from the plait into the trail. Keep these 2 pairs in the trail, making 2 extra pairs on the inner side and leave them out again for the plait at pin B. Follow Note 14 to take them into the trail at pin A.

The 2 pairs left out at pin X on the left-hand side of the centre trail make the leaf to pin Z on the right-hand side of the crossed trails. Make this leaf and take the pairs into that trail, following Note 13b.iv.

Return to right-hand trail

Work the trail pins until pin E. The pairs from the leaves at pins E and G work through the trail and are used for the plait pairs at pins F and H. Work to the right following Note 16a and Fig 52.

Crossing the trails at pins J, d, e and f

Follow Note 20b to cross the trails at pins J, d, e and f (Fig 52). Enclose pin f with a whole stitch and leave the weaver pairs here to make the leaf. Use the inner passive pairs next to pin f as the new weaver pairs for the trails and work them separately until the next crossing.

Ground plaits

These plaits have picots set opposite each other on either side of the plait (N2c). Work windmill crossings in the ground when 2 plaits or a plait and leaf meet (N9a).

The plaits from the ground enter the crossing trail on the right-hand side and work through to the left to make pairs for the leaves between the crossing trails (N16b and Fig 53).

Ground leaves

Work in and out of the centre trail (N13b.ii). The centre trail is connected to the right-hand crossing trail once more by a leaf – on the opposite side of the mat to pin Z. Follow Note 13b.iv to connect this leaf, to the right-hand crossing trail, as at pin Z.

Finishing

Centre trail. The pairs from the plaits work into the trail at the pins marked ⊙. They make extra pairs; remove threads to accommodate them (N15). Fasten the passive pairs into the loops left on the pin and the weaver pair into pin 1. The last leaf Q fastens into pin X (Fig 51).

Outer trails. The 4 passive pairs and the weaver pair each side fasten into the 5 loops left on the pins each side. The pairs from the outer plait fasten into pin A. Pairs from leaf K fasten into pin 3 and pairs from plaits M and N fasten into pins 18 and 22.

PATTERN 13   A HANDKERCHIEF CORNER MOTIF

34 pairs of bobbins wound in Campbell's linen 100, or B.O.U.C. linen 100.
An exercise in crossing trails.

Working notes (see Part III)

Trails. 1 weaver pair and 3 passive pairs.

   Outer plait. 4 pairs.

   Plaits and leaves. 8 pairs on the right; 10 new pairs for the centre area on the left.

N20a: Crossing trails.

N13b.ii: Plait pairs entering and leaving immediately same side.

N14: Plait and leaf pairs taken into the trails and not leaving immediately.

N16: Plait and leaf pairs working through the trails.

N3: Double picots.

N9: Windmill crossing.

N12: Eight-pair crossing.

N11: Six-pair crossing on the left at pin *R*.

Pattern 13

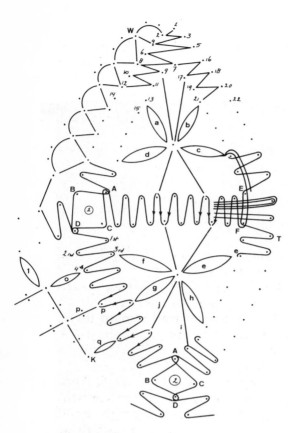

Figure 54
Pattern 13. Guide to setting in and working the first section.

Setting in

Follow Figs 54 and 55. Hang 8 pairs open round pin *1* (N8) – twist each pair once.

Use the second pair from the right as the weaver and work in whole stitch through the 6 passive pairs on the left, to pin *2* – do not twist the weaver pair. Set in 2 new pairs at pin *2* (N13b.i). Leave the weaver pair and the new right-hand pair out at pin *2* to make the plait to pin *W*. Take the new left-hand pair as the weaver pair to pin *3*. Twist it once – put up pin *3* and work back to pin *4*. Set in 2 new pairs at pin *4* (N13b.i). Leave the weaver pair and the new right-hand pair at pin *4* to make the plait to pin *W*, working a windmill crossing at pin *W*.

Working the trails

The left-hand trail

Take the new left-hand pair as the weaver pair and work to pins *5* and *6*. Take the weaver pair through 4 passive pairs only to pin *7* (see Fig 55). The pairs split into 2 trails at pin *7*. Put up pin *7* and enclose it with the weaver pair and the inner left-hand passive pair. This passive pair will now be on the right-hand side – it becomes the weaver pair in the right-hand trail – take it in whole stitch through 3 passive pairs – twist it once – put up pin *16*. Leave this pair behind pin *16* and leave the 3 passive pairs on the right. Put these pairs to the far right of the pillow.

Take the left-hand pair from pin *7* as the weaver pair in the left-hand trail. Work through 3 passive pairs to pin *8*. Take in the plait pairs at pin *8* (N13b.ii). Work the new weaver pair to pin *9* through the 3 passive pairs. Set in 2 new pairs at pin *9* (N13b.iii) and Fig 54. Leave the weaver pair and the new left-hand pair to make the plait from pin *9*. Take the new right-hand pair as the weaver pair in the trail and work to pin *13*, taking in the outer plait pairs at appropriate pin-holes. Twist the weaver pair once around pins at which no pairs enter or leave. Set in 2 new pairs at pin *13* and leave out the weaver pair and the left-hand new pair to make leaf *a* (N13b.iii). Continue the trail and outer plaits until the pin at which the pairs from leaf *d* are taken into the trail. Leave the weaver pair ready to work this pin.

The right-hand trail

Work the weaver pair from pin *16* to pin *17* and set in 2 new pairs at pin *17* (N13b.i). Leave out the weaver pair and new right-hand pair for the plait, and take the new left-hand pair as the weaver pair. Set pins *18*, *19* and *20* and set in 2 new pairs at pin *21* (N13b.i). The weaver pair and the new right-hand pair are left out at pin *21* to make leaf *b*. Take the left-hand new pair as the weaver pair and work as far as the pin at which the pairs from leaf *c* are taken into the trail. Make the plaits and leaves *a* and *b* – work an 8-pair crossing in the centre (N12) and then make the plaits and leaves *c* and *d*.

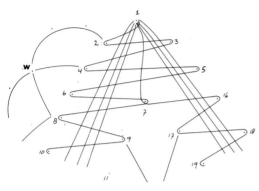

Figure 55
Guide to setting in – showing working
from pin *1* to pin *7*. Pairs are indicated
by single lines.

Return to the left-hand trail

Take in the 2 pairs from leaf *d* (N14) and remove 4 threads from the trail (N15) as the 2 extra pairs make the trail too bulky for the crossing. Work this trail and the outer plaits as far as pin *A* at Crossing 1. Bring the weaver pair to pin *A* at Crossing 1 – twist once and leave it here (see Fig 54).

Return to the right-hand trail

Take in the 2 pairs from leaf *c* (N14) – retain 1 pair in the trail to make 4 passive pairs and remove 2 threads to accommodate the other pair (N15). Work the trail as far as pin *E*. Twist the weaver pair once – put up pin *E* – do not enclose it – leave the weaver pair here behind pin *E*.

Setting in and working the cross-trail

Hang 2 pairs of bobbins open round the first pin marked ⊙ on Fig 57 (N8). Twist each pair once. Hang 1 pair of bobbins on the second pin marked ⊙. Now follow Fig 56. Work each one of these 3 pairs in whole stitch through the 4 pairs of trail passives. These 3 new pairs make the passive pairs in the centre trail. The passive pairs in the right-hand trail remain there. Bring the weaver pair from behind pin *E* in whole stitch through the 3 new passive pairs of the centre trail towards pin *F*. Twist this weaver pair once and put up pin *F* – leave this pair to the left-hand side of pin *F*.

Twist once the passive pair lying to the right-hand side of pin *F*. Work a whole stitch in front of pin *F* with this passive pair and the weaver pair. Twist both pairs once. There are now 3 pairs of passives in the right-hand trail – bring the right-hand pair from pin *F* in whole stitch through these 3 passive pairs – twist it once and put up pin *T*. Leave this weaver pair behind pin *T* and put it and the 3 passive pairs to the far right of the pillow.

Turn the pillow for easier working and take the left-hand pair from pin *F* through the 3 passive pairs in the centre trail and set pins *1*, *2* and *3* in this trail, twisting the weaver pair once round these pins. Work to pin *4* – twist the weaver pair once – put up pin *4* and leave the weaver pair behind this pin. From pin *5* to pin *12* work the plait pairs through the trail (follow Note 16 for pairs working through to the right). Finish working the centre trail to pin *A* at Crossing 1 (see Fig 54).

Trail crossings

Crossing 1.

Cross the trails at pins *A*, *B*, *C* and *D* by following instructions in Note 20a. Leave the left-hand pair at pin *D* to become the weaver pair in the left-hand outer trail.

Working the centre trail from Crossing 1

Follow Fig 54. Take the right-hand pair from pin *D* as the weaver pair in the centre trail and set the first 2 trail pins, twisting the weaver pair once

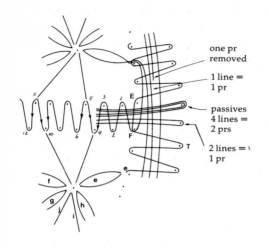

one pr
removed

1 line =
1 pr

passives
4 lines =
2 prs

2 lines = ›
1 pr

round them. At the third trail pin set in 2 new pairs, leaving out the weaver pair and the new left-hand pair for the leaf *f* (Fig 54). Take the new right-hand pair as the weaver pair to the fourth trail pin and set in 2 more new pairs. Follow Notes 13b.i & iii to set in the new pairs on the left and right. Leave out the weaver pair and the right-hand new pair to make the leaf *o*. Take the left-hand new pair as the weaver pair and work as far as the pin at which the plait *p* is left out. Twist the weaver pair once – put up pin *p* and leave the weaver pair behind it. Leave the centre trail at this pin.

Return to the right-hand trail

Bring the weaver pair from pin *T* and work the trail to pin *e* (Figs 56, 54). Set in 2 new pairs at pin *e* (N13b.i). The weaver pair and the right-hand new pair remain out for the leaf and the left-hand new pair becomes the weaver pair in the trail. Make the plaits and the leaves *e* and *f* – work an 8-pair crossing (N12) in the centre and make the plaits *i* and *j* and the leaves *g* and *h*.

Figure 56
Working the cross-trail.

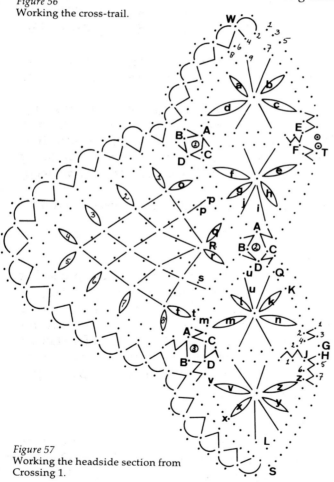

Figure 57
Working the headside section from Crossing 1.

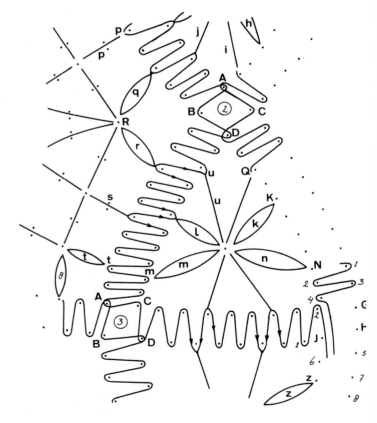

Figure 58
Working the trail at Crossings 2 & 3.

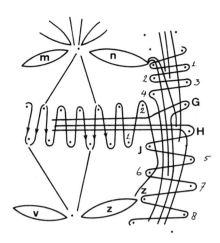

Figure 59
Finishing at pins *J*, *G* & *H*.
Passive pairs are indicated by single lines.

Continue the right-hand trail, twisting the weaver pair once round the pins. Take in the pairs from leaf *h* and plait *i* at the appropriate pin-holes (N14), removing threads from the trail (N15) to accommodate them.

Work the weaver pair to pin *A* at Crossing 2 (Figs 54 and 57) and leave it there after twisting it once.

Return to the centre trail

Follow Note 16b to take the pairs from leaf *g* and plait *j* through the trail to the left – to leave out pairs on the left-hand side for plait *p* and leaf *q* (Fig 54). Finish the trail to pin *A* at Crossing 2 – twist the weaver pair once and cross the trails at pins *A*, *B*, *C* and *D* (N20a). Make pin *D* and leave the trails at this pin.

Working trail, outer plait and headside section from Crossing 1

Bring the weaver pair from pin *D* (Fig 57) – work the trail and the outer plait, taking in the pairs from the outer plait at appropriate pin-holes and, at the same time, setting in 2 new pairs on the right-hand side (N13b.iii) at appropriate pin-holes to make the leaves *1*, *2*, *3* and *4*; 8 pairs will be needed altogether.

Work the trial and outer plait until the pin is reached at which the pairs from leaf *5* are taken into the trail. Leave the weaver pair ready to work this pin.

Make all the leaves and plaits in the centre using windmill crossings (N9) where 4 pairs meet, and one 6-pair crossing at pin *R* (N11). After working these, anchor the leaf pairs until they are taken up into their appropriate pin-holes. Work the left-hand trail as far as pin *A* at Crossing 3 (Fig 57), taking in the pairs from leaves *5*, *6*, *7* and *8* (N14) and removing threads to accommodate them (N15).

Note. The trail should have only its original number of passive pairs for the crossing.

Return to the centre trail at Crossing 2

Use the left-hand pair at pin *D* as the weaver pair and work to pin *u* (Fig 58). Twist the weaver pair once – put up pin *u* and leave the weaver pair behind this pin. Follow Note 16 to work the pairs from leaf *r* and plait *s* through the trail to the right – to leave out pairs on the right-hand side for plait *u* and leaf *l*. Work the trail to pin *t* and remove 2 threads before taking in the 2 pairs from leaf *t* (N15). Follow instructions in Note 14 to take in the leaf pairs and remove 2 more threads before taking the weaver pair to pin *m*. This will accommodate the pairs from leaf *t*.

Working the right-hand trail from Crossing 2

Take the right-hand pair from pin *D* (Fig 58) as the weaver pair and work the right-hand trail as far as pin *N*, setting in 2 new pairs at pin *Q* and 2 new pairs at pin *K*, and leaving out pairs for the leaf and plait. Make the

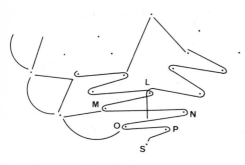

Figure 60
Finishing at pins *L* & *S*.

plaits and the leaves *k* and *l* – work the centre crossing of 8 pairs and make the plaits and leaves *m* and *n*. Take the 2 pairs from leaf *n* into the right-hand trail, removing 4 threads to accommodate them. Make the next 4 trail pins and leave the weaver pair behind pin 4 after twisting it once.

Return to the centre trail

Take up the pairs from leaf *m* (N14, Fig 58). Work back across the trail and then lay the inner pair from leaf *m* to the back of the pillow. When the bobbins of this pair are cut off leave thread long enough to pass into a needle as these ends *must* be woven into the lace when it is completed. The usual procedure of removing threads and trimming close to the lace cannot be followed here due to the extra numbers of pairs coming in at *t* and *m*.

Work the trail to pin *A* of Crossing 3. Remove 2 more threads before working the crossing.

Working Crossing 3 and lower cross-trail

Follow Note 20a and Fig 58 to cross the trails at this point. Take the right-hand pair from *D* as the weaver pair in the centre trail and work as far as pin *J*, taking the plait pairs through the trail as before from right to left (N16). Leave the weaver pair at pin *J*. Take the left-hand pair from pin *D* as the weaver pair in the left-hand trail and work as far as pin *x* (Fig 57), setting in 2 new pairs and leaving out 2 pairs (N13b.iii) for the leaf at pin *v*.

Finishing

At pins J, G and H

Refer to Fig 59. The weaver pair from the right-hand trail should be left behind pin 4, after twisting it. The weaver pair from the centre trail should be left at pin *J*. Do not twist this pair – put up pin *J* – do not enclose the pin.

Take the first passive pair from the centre trail through the weaver pair at pin 4 and through the 3 passive pairs of the right-hand trail. Twist this pair once and put up pin *G*. Bring the pair back through 2 passive pairs only. Leave it as a passive pair in the right-hand trail. This makes 5 passive pairs.

Bring the second passive pair from the centre trail through the 5 passive pairs to pin *H*. Twist this pair once – put up pin *H* and leave this pair behind pin *H*. Remove 2 threads from the right-hand trail pairs. Throughout the work here, choose carefully the threads to be removed – selecting those that have been in the trail the longest. There will now be 4 passive pairs in the right-hand trail.

Bring the third passive pair from the centre trail through the 4 passive pairs and leave it as a passive pair on the right of the trail in front of pin *H*. This will make 5 passive pairs. Take the weaver pair from pin *H* through the 5 passive pairs to pin *J*. Remove pin *J* and work a whole stitch through the weaver pair from the centre trail. Put up pin *J* between this

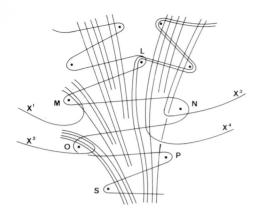

Figure 61
Finishing the lace and removing threads. Threads marked x are used to tie the bundle back over the lace.

pair and the pair from pin H, which should be twisted once. Remove 2 threads. Bring the weaver pair from pin J through 5 passive pairs to pin 5 – twist it once – put up pin 5 and work to pin 6 through 5 pairs. Twist the weaver pair once – remove 2 threads from the trail – put up pin 6 and work to pin 7 through 4 passive pairs. Twist the weaver pair once and put up pin 7. Work to pin z through 3 passive pairs only, leaving the fourth passive pair out of the trail at pin 6. Set in one new pair at pin z (N13a). Leave this new pair out of the trail at pin z. Take the weaver pair to pin 8 – twist it once and put up pin 8. Leave the trail at pin 8.

The pairs left out from pins 6 and z make leaf z. Make the leaves v and z and the 2 plaits – work the 8-pair crossing and make the plaits and leaves x and y (see Fig 57).

Work both trails as far as pin L, taking in the pairs from the plait and leaf on each side (N14), removing threads in each trail to accommodate these pairs (N15).

Finishing at pins L to S
Refer to Figs 60 and 61. The weaver pairs from each trail meet at pin L. Work a whole stitch with them – put up pin L – enclose with a whole stitch but do not twist the pairs. The 2 trails now merge again (see Fig 60). Leave the right-hand pair at pin L as a passive pair in the centre and take the left-hand pair to pin M as the weaver pair. Take in the plait pairs at pin M (N14). Remove 2 threads from each trail to the back of the pillow. Work from pin M to pin N through 7 passive pairs. Put up pin N and remove 2 threads to the back of the pillow. Remove one thread from the left *(x1)* and one from the right *(x2)* and lay these 2 threads to the left and right sides of the pillow (Fig 61). These threads will be needed later to tie the last threads back across the lace.

Work from pin N to pin O through 5 passive pairs and take in the 2 pairs from the last plait. Remove 2 threads to the back of the pillow. Remove one more thread from the right *(x4)* and left *(x3)*, to the sides of the pillow (Fig 61). These will also be needed later to tie with. Work to pin P through 5 passive pairs. Put up pin P and remove 2 threads to the back of the pillow. Work to pin S through 4 passive pairs – put up pin S – work one more row through these pairs. Tie the weaver pair tightly, with a reef knot, against threads to form a bundle. Push all pins down out of the way.

Take the 2 outside threads of the bundle underneath it and cross them over. Bring them back over the top and tie in a reef knot over the bundle. Lay these 2 threads back with the bundle. Turn the whole bundle back over the lace between the end pins. Use the 2 sets of threads (*x1* and *x2*; *x3* and *x4*) laid to the left and right sides of the pillow after working pins N and O to tie the bundle back over the lace. Trim these threads close to the bundle. Cut off all bobbins, remove the pins and lift the lace.

Trim all threads close to the lace except the 2 from leaf m. These must be woven into the trail with a needle.

65

PATTERN 14   A FOUR CORNER MOTIF

Suitable for a paper-weight, for framing or for mounting in the lid of a trinket box.

21 pairs of bobbins wound in Bocken's linen 80.

A final exercise in the techniques studied in this book.

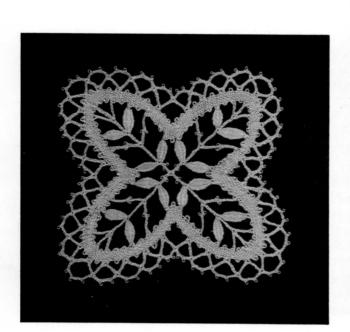

Pattern 14

Working notes (see Part III)

Headside. Four pairs making 2 plaits, the outer plait with single picots set to the left. Windmill crossings are worked whenever the plaits meet.

Trail. Four passive pairs and a weaver. The trail gains on a pin at the centre curves (N17a).

The ground. Four pairs will make the 'stalks' A and B into the centre which will windmill and then make the 2 'stalks' C and D out from the centre.

The leaves and plaits work out from the trail, through the plait 'stalk', and into the trail on the other side. Of these 8 pairs, 6 pairs are taken into the trail and other threads removed to accommodate them. New pairs must be set in each time. The 2 pairs near the centre can be kept in for the short distance round the bottom of the curve and then left out again.

Before finishing all the pairs will be accommodated into the trail except for the leaf entering at pin 4. These 2 pairs will fasten off here.

Set in the trail at pins *1* and *2* and work pins *3* and *4*. Work to pin *5*, leave the weaver pair here and gain on the pin.

Set in 2 new pairs (N13b.iii) at each of the pins *7*, *13*, *19* and *23*. Set in 2 new pairs for the plait 'stalk' at pin *27*.

Set in the pairs for the outer plait at pin *10* and work this in the usual way.

Figure 62
Pattern 14. Guide to pin-holes.

Glossary

Enclosing a pin. Making a further stitch in front of a pin, after setting it into the pin-hole, with the same two pairs. See Part I, p. 4.

Edge pair. A pair which forms the outer limit on the footside, continually changing places with the weaver pair. Each time a foot pin is set the edge pair becomes the weaver pair and the weaver pair becomes the edge pair for the next edge pin. See Part I, p. 7.

Fastening off. Joining the threads at the end of the lace to the beginning. See Part I, p. 8.

Footside. The straight edge of the lace, usually worked on the right-hand side in English lace, which is attached to the mounting material.

Ground. The area between the footside and the headside. In Bedfordshire lace this is made up with plaits, leaves and half-stitch trails and circles.

Half-stitch. The first 2 movements of a whole stitch. See Part I, p. 4.

Headside. The outer edge of the lace, often curved, opposite the footside. In English lace this is normally worked on the left-hand side.

Leaf. An elongated shape made with 2 pairs of bobbins by weaving one thread under and over the other three. Also known as woven plaits, wheatears or petals. See Part III, p. 6.

Ninepin. An arrangement of plaited pairs on the headside, characteristic of Bedfordshire lace.

Passive pairs. Pairs which remain in the working area with the threads running vertically in the lace.

Picot. The decorative loop on the plait. See Part III, p. 3.

Plait. Continuous braid made with 2 pairs working half-stitches. Also known as 'legs' or 'bars'. See Part III, p. 3.

Pricking. The pin-hole pattern pricked into a piece of card or parchment from which the lace is worked.

Putting up a pin. See Setting a pin.

Setting a pin. Inserting a pin into the appropriate pin-hole.

Setting in. Beginning a pattern or a section of a pattern.

Setting up the lace. Moving the lace up the pillow to work another section or turn a corner. See Part I, p. 2.

Stitch. The basic element of lace-making. A stitch is made by moving 2 pairs of bobbins in a specific way. There are 2 stitches used in lace-making: a whole stitch, also known as full stitch or cloth stitch, and a half-stitch. The vast intricacy of lace is achieved using these 2 stitches, weaving and twisting the bobbins in various ways. See Part I, p. 3.

Trail. A band of whole stitch or half-stitch which runs continuously throughout the lace, often on a curve.

Twist. The action of passing the right thread of a pair over the left.

Prickings

b c d e f

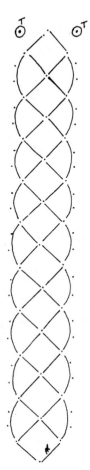

Pattern 1a

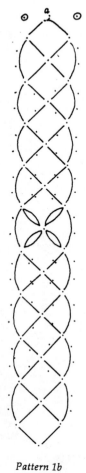

Pattern 1b

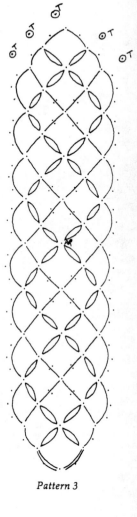

Pattern 3

Pattern A.
Practice band.

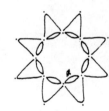

Pattern 2

Weaver pair. The working pair which weaves horizontally forwards and backwards across the passive pairs. See Fig 5.

Whole stitch. The basic stitch of lace-making made with 2 pairs of bobbins. For detailed description see p. 3.

Windmill crossing. The particular movement of threads when 4 pairs meet at one pin-hole. For detailed description see Part III, p. 8.

Reading List

Buck, A., Thomas Lester, his lace and the East Midlands Industry 1820–1905, Ruth Bean, Bedford, 1981

Freeman, C.E., Pillow Lace in the East Midlands, Luton Museum and Art Gallery, 1958

Hamer, M., Pillow Lace, Book 2: English Maltese type lace edging with corners, Margaret Hamer, Bedford, 1977

Levey, S.M., Lace, A history, Victoria and Albert Museum/W.S. Maney & Son Ltd, London/Leeds, 1983

Wright, T., The Romance of the Lace Pillow, Olney, 1919; reprint, Ruth Bean, Bedford, 1982

Prickings

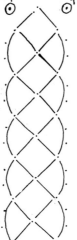

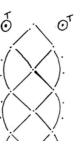

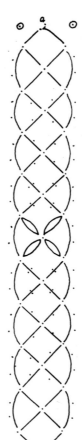

Pattern 1a

Pattern 1b

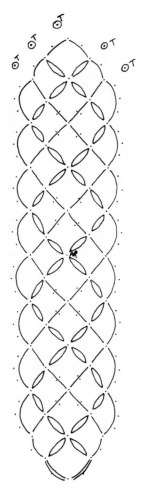

Pattern 3

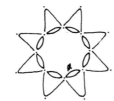

Pattern 2

Pattern A.
Practice band.

70

Pattern 4

Pattern 5

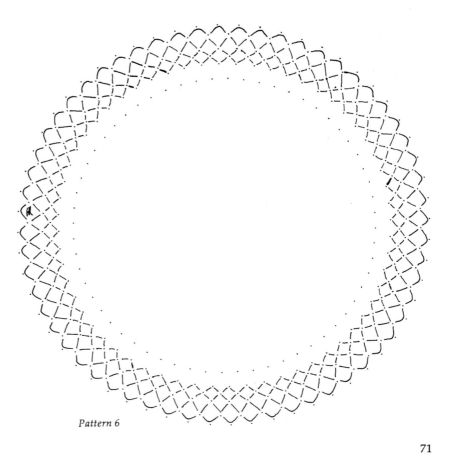

Pattern 6

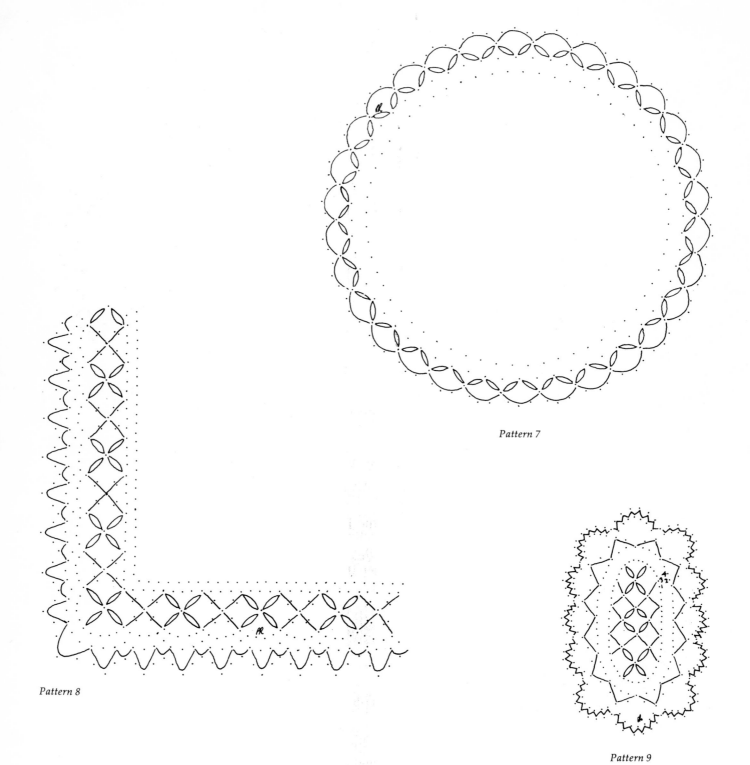

Pattern 7

Pattern 8

Pattern 9

Pattern 11

Pattern 10

Pattern 13

Pattern 12

Pattern 14

Part III

WORKING NOTES FOR THE PATTERNS

The Working Notes are arranged in the order they are first required but most are used for working several patterns. Before the Notes, two diagrams are given which illustrate the construction of typical Bedfordshire lace patterns and the principal techniques used to work them. These techniques are explained in detail in the Working Notes.

DIAGRAMS OF TWO TYPICAL BEDFORDSHIRE PATTERNS

Numbers and letters are used in the diagrams to indicate important points in the patterns. The Table below shows these numbers and letters in the left-hand column. Opposite them are shown the titles of the corresponding Working Notes, with their numbers and page numbers in the right-hand columns.

Key to diagrams codes and notes

Code		Note	Page
	Basic elements		
P	Plaits	1	3
p	Picots: on the headside, set to the left – a. single	2a–b	3
	b. double	3a–b	5
	on the ground plait, set facing each other	2c, 3c	4, 5
	on the curve of a plait	2d, 3d	4, 6
L	Leaf	4	6
	Headside : trail and ninepin		
1	Set in the trail weaver pair on this pin (see Pattern 4).		
2–5	Trail pins (see Pattern 4).		
T	Temporary pin	5	7
	Trail passive pairs are hung in order on this pin when setting in the lace.	7	7
A	Two new pairs are set into one pin-hole on the left of the trail.	13b.i	12
B	Two new pairs are set into a plait by a windmill crossing.	9b	10
	Incorporates hanging pairs open round a pin.	8	8
C	A crossing of plaits on the ninepin	9a	10
D	Plait pairs are worked into one pin-hole on the left of the trail and leave immediately on the same side (see Pattern 4).	13b.ii	13
W	Windmill crossing: 4 pairs meet at one pin-hole.	9a	10
6	Gaining on a trail pin and taking in plait pairs.	17b	18
7	Two new pairs are set into one pin-hole on the right of the trail.	13b.iii	14

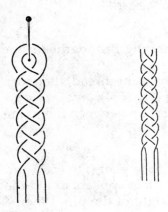

Figure 63
Plaits.
Ease up after making each of the
half-stitches.

Note 1. Plaits

The plait is made with 2 pairs of bobbins working continuous half-stitch (Fig 63). Tension is achieved by easing up the half-stitches firmly, but not tightly as the plait must lie flat. If pulled too tightly it can pucker or twist; but if not eased tightly enough 'holes' can appear between the half-stitches.

Begin by making 2 half-stitches – ease these up so that the plait nestles against the starting pin. Continue making half-stitches one after the other, easing each one up so that it lies firmly against the previous one.

The length of the plait is determined by the distance between the pin-holes at which it begins and is to end. The last half-stitch of the plait should be made just at the pin-hole where it is required to end. If a plait is joined into the next part of the work and seems to be twisting upwards or away from the pin and is not lying flat, it has probably been made one half-stitch too long. Undo the connecting pin and then undo one half-stitch from the plait before re-joining it to the work.

Note 2. Picots

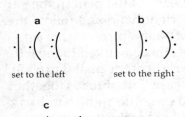

a   b

set to the left   set to the right

c

on both sides
facing or staggered

Figure 64
Single picots.

A picot is the decorative loop found on the plait. It can be worked on only one side of the plait – to the right or to the left, or on both sides – staggered or facing each other (see Fig 64a-c).

The picot is made with only one of the 2 pairs of bobbins that make the plait. If the picot is set to the left-hand side it is worked with the left-hand pair of bobbins; set to the right it is worked with the right-hand pair.

Single or double picots can be made (see Note 3 below). The single, or Continental, picot is made on only one thread of the pair; the double picot is made with both threads. Traditionally, Bedfordshire lace was made with double picots in order to distinguish the hand-made lace from that made by machine, since double picots could not be reproduced on the machines. Today, while following the established traditions of lace-making, we can chose more by individual preference since we no longer compete with machines.

As a general guide single picots are easier to make with thicker threads such as linen 80, but double picots should be made with finer threads such as DMC 50. Some threads, such as the DMC 30 or Campbell's linen 100, will work either type just as well. In this book the first 2 patterns introduce single picots and the third pattern uses the double picot. The remaining patterns show picots according to the above general thread guide.

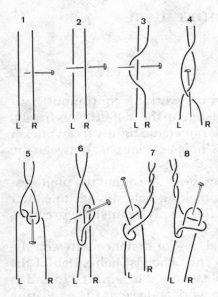

Figure 65
Working single picots set to the left or to the right.
7. Completed picots, set to the left.
8. Completed picots, set to the right.

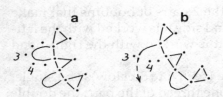

Figure 66
Picots set on the curve of plaits.
b. Continue to work the plait in the direction of the dotted line, before curving it round, to avoid irregularity.

a. Single picots set to the left of a plait

Take the 2 left-hand bobbins of the plait in the left hand and hold them taut. Take a pin in the right hand and work as follows:

★Put it under the right of the 2 threads with the point of the pin away from you (Fig 65:1).

Take it over the left thread (Fig 65:2).

Pull the left thread across towards you bringing it underneath the right (Fig 65:3).

Bring the pin towards you and back over the right thread, then turn the point of the pin down and away from you (Fig 65:4).

Take it under the crossed threads and bring it up between them (Fig 65:5).

The picot loop is now on the pin (Fig 65:6).★

Pin this loop into the pin-hole on the left of the plait (Fig 65:7) and ease both threads together until a single tight picot appears round the pin. Both pairs of the plait should be on the right of the pin. When a picot is made the plait pair becomes untwisted so the left-hand pair should now be twisted once before continuing to work the plait. Make sure that the half-stitches are well eased up against the picot pin otherwise a 'hole' can appear in the plait near the picot.

b. Single picots set to the right of a plait

Follow Fig 65: 1-6. Take the 2 right-hand threads of the plait in the left hand and hold them taut. Take a pin in the right hand and follow the instructions ★ to ★ above, for working the left-hand picot. Picots set to the right are made in exactly the same way as those worked to the left.

Pin the picot loop into the pin-hole on the right of the plait (Fig 65:8), keeping both pairs to the left of the pin, and ease both threads together until a single tight picot appears round the pin. The right-hand pair should now be twisted once before continuing to make the plait.

c. Single picots set facing each other on either side of a plait

Work one picot and twist the pair that made it once (Fig 64c). Work one half-stitch with both pairs. Work the other picot and twist the pair that made it once. Continue making the plait.

d. Single picots set on the curve of a plait

An example of picots set on a curve is given in Fig 66a. As the plait curves round from the picot pin, a hole can appear in it near the picot, or the picot can become too long and loose and the plait seems to pull away from it. This can be avoided by making sure that the half-stitches of the plait are well pulled up after the picots are made and also by continuing to make the plait in a straight line for a little way before curving it round.

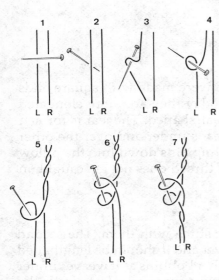

Figure 67
Working double picots, set to the left.

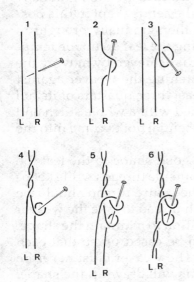

Figure 68
Working double picots set to the right.

For example, after making picot 3 of the curved plait in Fig 66b, working of the plait should continue in the direction indicated by the dotted line. Turn it into the curve when it is long enough to make the next picot – 4.

Note 3. Double picots

a. Double picots set to the left of a plait

Follow Fig 67. The left-hand pair of the plait should be twisted 3 times before making the picot. Hold the 2 left-hand bobbins of the plait pair taut in the left hand. Then:

1. Take a pin in the right hand and holding it away from you, with the point towards the left, put it over the top of the left thread.

2. Move the pin down towards the left and bring it back under the thread towards you.

3. Keep the thread over the pin.

4. Take the pin back over the thread away from you.

5. The picot loop is now on the pin. Set the loop into the picot pin-hole keeping it slack.

6. Take the right-hand thread of the pair round behind the pin clockwise and replace it to the right of the left-hand thread. Ease both threads together tightly round the pin. It is essential to ease both threads together or the picot will split.

7. Twist the threads twice right over left. Continue to work the plait making sure that the half-stitches are well eased up against the pin.

b. Double picots set to the right of a plait

Follow Fig 68. You must twist the right-hand pair of the plait 3 times. Hold the 2 right-hand bobbins taut. Then:

1. Take a pin in the right hand holding it with the point towards the left – put it under the right-hand thread.

2. Bring the pin over the thread towards you.

3. Turn the pin down and back keeping the thread round it.

4. The picot loop is now on the pin. Set this loop into the picot pin-hole keeping the thread slack.

5. Take the left-hand thread of the pair round behind the pin anti-clockwise and bring it back into place on the inside of the right-hand thread.

Ease both threads tightly round the pin together.

6. Twist the pair twice, right over left.

Continue working the plait, making sure that the half-stitches are well pulled up against the pin.

c. Double picots set facing each other on either side of a plait

Follow Note 2c but work double picots.

Figure 69
Structure of a leaf.

move outer threads further apart

outer threads gradually brought back to centre

Figure 70
Shaping leaves.

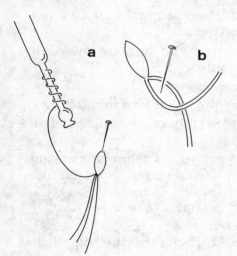

Figure 71
Working leaves.
a. Lay weaver to back of pillow.
b. Anchor pairs temporarily.

d. Double picots set on the curve of a plait
Follow Note 2d but work double picots.

Note 4. Leaves
In old Bedfordshire Maltese lace, leaves were made with square ends giving the appearance of a rectangle. Today they are more elongated with pointed ends and look distinctly leaf-shaped. The leaf is formed with 2 pairs by weaving one of the threads under and over the other three. It is a good idea to push surrounding pins down into the pillow while making a leaf so that the weaving thread does not get caught on them.

Making the leaf
Twist each pair once and work a whole stitch with them. The second thread from the right is used as the weaver and it should be lengthened slightly so that it does not catch on the other bobbins as it weaves under and over the threads. Weave in the following manner; take it under the bobbin on the right – back over it – under the centre thread – over and under the thread on the left – back over the centre thread – under and over the right-hand thread and so on (Fig 69).

The finished shape of the leaf depends entirely on the position of the 2 outside threads as it is being made. At the start of the leaf the 3 threads are kept fairly close together. The 2 outside threads are then gradually moved further apart to widen the shape in the centre, kept in this position for most of the length of the leaf and then gradually brought in again to form the point (Fig 70). When making the leaf do not be tempted to come into a point too soon. The shape is achieved by moving the 2 outside threads slowly inwards and tightening the weaver against them, but the leaf should have reached at least three quarters of its full length before this is done. The leaf is finished with a whole stitch and this tends to draw it up too. It is therefore essential not to come into the point too soon.

Points to remember. In order to achieve a good shape to the leaf the weaving thread has to be eased against the outside threads while keeping these threads away from the centre. The centre thread should be kept taut down the middle. After lifting each thread to take the weaver under and over, replace it in its original position to maintain the shape. At the same time the weaver thread has to be eased up so that each weave across lies next to the one before it. The weaver must never be allowed to drop forward or to tighten as this will draw up the shape. Great care must be taken when making the finishing whole stitch; many beautifully shaped leaves have been spoilt at this point!

If the leaf is to be laid aside before being brought back into the work, it is a good idea to place the weaver thread over the back of the pillow to prevent the thread dropping and pulling the leaf out of shape (Fig

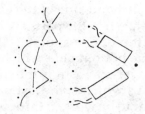

Figure 72
Leaves worked with pairs that come
from 2 pin-holes.

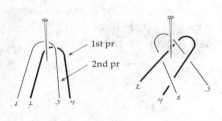

1st pr
2nd pr

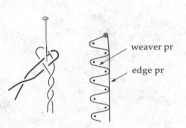

weaver pr

edge pr

Figure 73
Hanging 2 pairs at one pin-hole.

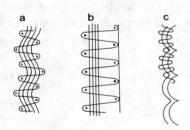

a   b   c

Figure 74
Hanging pairs in order on a pin.
a. Trail passives.
b. Footside passives.
c. Scallop passives.

71a). Sometimes a pin can be placed in a convenient nearby pin-hole and the leaf anchored around it temporarily (Fig 71b). It is essential to keep the weaver slack until it is anchored into the next part of the work.

Leaves made from pairs which come from 2 separate pin-holes are made in exactly the same way. The 2 top pairs are twisted once each and worked in a whole stitch before beginning to weave. They can have a square ended top when begun this way but must have the same shape at the bottom (Fig 72).

Note. When several leaves come together at one pin-hole a crossing is worked appropriate to the number of leaves (N9a, N11 and N12); but the pairs should not be twisted after the crossing – the second set of leaves begins with just a whole stitch.

HANGING BOBBINS ON A PIN

Note 5. Temporary pins

While setting in and working the lace new pairs have to be brought in as required. Temporary pins are used to hang these pairs on until they are worked into the lace. The temporary pin is placed in any convenient pin-hole near the one at which the new pair is needed. Once the new pair has been worked into the lace and is secured by the pin in the working pin-hole, the temporary pin should be removed and the new pair (or pairs) eased down into the lace.

Note 6. Setting in 2 pairs at one pin

This is most often used to set in the edge pair and the weaver pair at the footside (Fig 73).

Hang the first pair of bobbins round the pin. Hang the second pair so that the right-hand bobbin lies between the 2 bobbins of the first pair – the left-hand bobbin of the second pair lies to the far left, as shown in Fig 73. Work as follows: place bobbin 2 over 1; 4 over 3 and cross the 2 middle bobbins left over right. This makes a whole stitch round the pin.

The pairs are then twisted according to the thread size and the pin-hole spacing. As a guide, the right-hand pair is most often twisted 3 times and the left-hand pair once.

The right-hand pair becomes the edge pair and the left-hand pair becomes the weaver pair to the first inner pin-hole of the footside.

Note 7. Hanging pairs in order on a pin

This is used when setting in the passive pairs for trails, for the footside or at a headside scallop (Fig 74).

The bobbins are hung on a temporary pin so that the 2 bobbins of one pair lie next to each other. The 2 bobbins of the next pair lie next to each other either to the right or to the left of the first pair. The 2 bobbins of the third pair lie next to the 2 bobbins of the second pair, and so on.

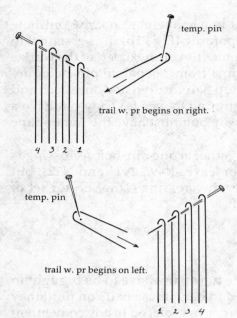

temp. pin

trail w. pr begins on right.

4 3 2 1

temp. pin

trail w. pr begins on left.

1 2 3 4

Figure 75
Hanging pairs in order on a temporary pin.

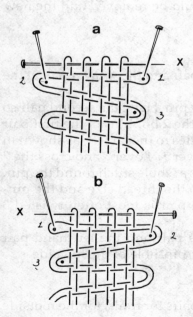

a

x

2   1

3

b

x

1

2

3

Figure 76
Hanging pairs in order.
Pin marked x is the temporary pin laid back with loops.
a. Weaver pair begins on the right.
b. Weaver pair begins on the left.

8

If the weaver pair begins from a pin on the left-hand side of the trail then the passives are hung in order from the left. When the pairs are on the temporary pin they appear to be lying on top of one another. The bobbins of the pairs should be placed so that the bottom pair, which is the first pair put on, is lying nearest to the weaver pair as it is the first pair to be worked through (Fig 75). The top pair, which is the last pair to be put on the temporary pin and is the last pair to be worked through, should be lying farthest away from the weaver pair. If the weaver pair begins from a pin on the right-hand side of the trail then the passive pairs are hung in order from the right; the first pair lies on the right and the last pair will be to the left-hand side.

After the weaver pair has worked one or 2 rows through the passives the temporary pin is lifted carefully, keeping the loops on it, and is laid back across the pillow behind the first 2 pins (Fig 76). The passive pairs are eased down into the lace as the loops must not be left too long. When the lace is completed the passive pairs fasten off into these loops.

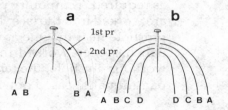

a   b
1st pr
2nd pr

A B   B A   A B C D   D C B A

Figure 77
Hanging pairs open on a pin.

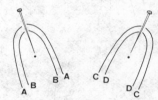

A B   B A   C D   D C

Figure 78
Four pairs, to be worked in a windmill crossing.

Note 8. Hanging pairs open round a pin

This is used when setting in 2 new pairs into one pin-hole of the existing work (Fig 77a) or when setting in 4 pairs at one pin (Fig 77b).

The pairs are hung round the pin so that the 2 bobbins of the first pair lie next to each other; the remaining pairs fall one bobbin on each side outside the first pair. The bobbins are then used in pairs, reading from the left:

AB – BA (Fig 77a)
AB – CD – DC – BA (Fig 77b)

CROSSING PAIRS
Note 9. Windmill crossings

A windmill crossing is a whole stitch worked in 2 stages and is used for the following:

    a. as a crossing whenever 4 pairs meet at one pin-hole;
    b. to set in 2 new pairs into a plait;

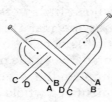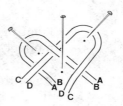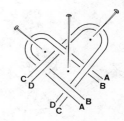

Figure 79
Windmill crossing.
Four pairs meeting at one pin-hole.

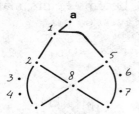

Figure 80
Section of Patterns 1a & 1b. A windmill crossing will be used to set in 2 new pairs into a plait, at pin 2 (or leaf tip in other patterns).

c. to set in 4 pairs at one pin-hole.

A windmill crossing is always worked with 4 pairs of bobbins, which are used as if they were only 2 pairs (2 threads are treated as one, see Fig 78). It is used where 2 plaits, 2 leaves, or a plait and leaf meet.

Treating 2 threads as one (Fig 78). The 2 threads A and B are treated as one thread. Threads B and A are treated as one. Then $AB - BA$ become 1 pair of bobbins instead of 2.

Threads C and D are treated as 1 thread. Threads D and C are treated as one. Then $CD - DC$ become 1 pair of bobbins instead of two.

Now there are only 2 pairs of bobbins working the crossing ($AB - BA$) ($CD - DC$) instead of four.

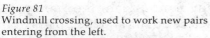

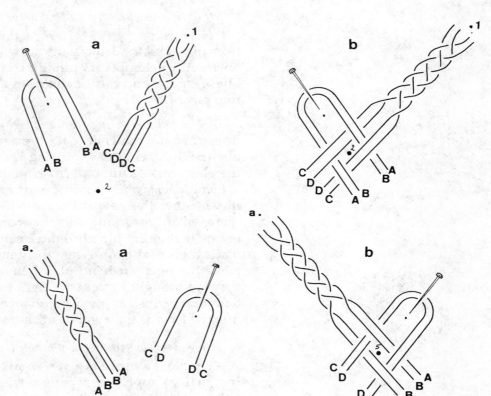

Figure 81
Windmill crossing, used to work new pairs entering from the left.
a. New pairs on temporary pin on the left.
b. Windmill crossing at pin 2.

Figure 82
Windmill crossing, used to work new pairs entering from the right.
a. New pairs on temporary pin on the right.
b. Windmill crossing at pin 5.

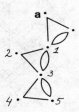

Figure 83
Section of Pattern 2.

Figure 84
Windmill crossing.
a. Four pairs open on temporary pin *a*.
b. & c. Working the windmill crossing into pin *1*.

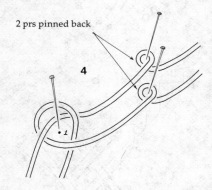

2 prs pinned back

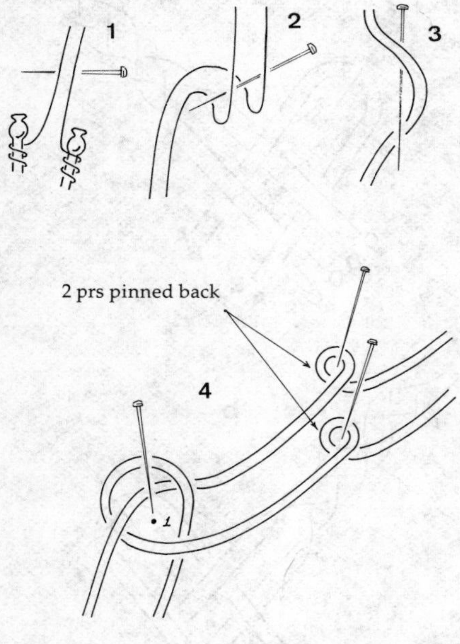

Figure 85
Pinning 2 pairs to the back of the pillow.

a. Four pairs meeting at one pin-hole (Fig 79)

This crossing is a whole stitch worked in 2 stages, as follows:
★Treating 2 threads as one, make the first 2 movements of a whole stitch (in effect – a half-stitch). Place *BA* over *CD* – pass *DC* over *BA* and place *CD* over *AB*. Set a pin between the pairs. There will be 4 threads on each side of the pin. Complete the windmill crossing by enclosing the pin with the last movement of a whole stitch. Pass *AB* over *DC*.★

After completing the windmill crossing the threads are treated singly again. *AB* – *BA* become 2 pairs again; *CD* – *DC* become 2 pairs, making the 4 pairs ready to work the next 2 plaits or leaves.

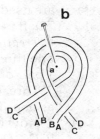

b. Setting in 2 new pairs into a plait or the tip of a leaf (Fig 80)

i. New pairs entering from the left. The existing plait has been made from pin *1* and the 2 new pairs are needed at pin *2*. Hang the 2 new pairs open round a temporary pin in a convenient nearby pin-hole (Fig 81a). These 2 pairs and the 2 pairs from the plait work a windmill crossing into pin *2* (Fig 81b).

ii. New pairs entering from the right (Fig 82). The plait has been made from pin *a* and the 2 new pairs are needed at pin *5*. Hang the 2 new pairs open round a temporary pin (Fig 82a). These 2 pairs and the 2 pairs from the plait work a windmill crossing into pin *5* (Fig 82b).

Point to remember. When 2 pairs are brought into an existing plait in this manner the new pairs are rather 'loose' if the temporary pin is removed after working only the windmill crossing. They are better left on the temporary pin until the 2 pairs already worked in the lace have made their next plait. When the new pairs are brought in from the left make the next left-hand plait before removing the temporary pin. If they are brought in from the right make the next right-hand plait. The temporary pins can then be removed and the new pairs eased down into the lace, as they will be anchored by the plait just made.

c. Setting in 4 new pairs at one pin-hole (Figs 83, 84)

A section of Pattern 2 is given as an example (Fig 83), but the following instructions apply to any pattern where 4 pairs are set in at one pin-hole to begin plaits or leaves.

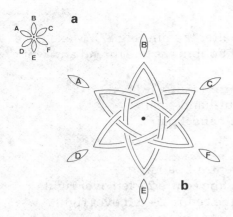

Figure 86
Six-pair crossing.
a. Three leaves before and three after the pin.
b. Detail of the crossing movement.

Figure 87
Eight-pair crossing.

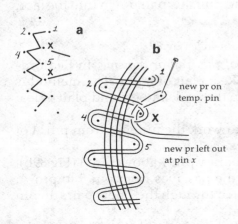

new pr on temp. pin

X

new pr left out at pin x

Figure 88
Setting in new pairs at trail and footside.
a. Pattern section.
b. Working diagram.

Set a temporary pin at *a* and hang the 4 pairs of bobbins open round it (Fig 84a). Make a windmill crossing to work the 4 pairs from the temporary pin into the starting pin-hole. Follow Fig 84b-c. Treat each 2 threads as one thread so that the crossing is made with only 2 pairs. Place threads *CD* over threads *DC*. Pass threads *DC* over threads *AB* and take threads *BA* over threads *CD*. Set pin *1* into the pin-hole so that there are 4 threads on each side of it. Finish the windmill crossing and enclose the pin by passing threads *AB* over threads *BA*.

When setting in 4 new pairs into a pattern in this way none are anchored by lace already made and are therefore all 'loose'. If the pairs are needed to make a plait and a leaf it is better to work the plait first. If they are intended for 2 plaits or 2 leaves, either one can be worked first. In any of these situations the following method (N10) can be used to anchor 2 pairs until one plait or leaf is made and is anchored elsewhere.

Note 10. Pinning 2 pairs to the back of the pillow

Hold the 2 bobbins of the pair to be laid back in the left hand. Take a pin in the right hand and put it under both threads (Fig 85:1). Bring it back over both threads (Fig 85:2) and take it down into the pillow, keeping the loop of both threads on the pin (Fig 85:3). Push the pin right down into the pillow. This anchors the pair (Fig 85:4). Pin the other pair back in the same way. Make the first plait or leaf with the other 2 pairs; anchor this round a temporary pin in a convenient pin-hole or work it into another area of the pattern before unpinning the pairs that were laid back.

CROSSING OF LEAVES

Note 11. Six-pair crossing

Three leaves are worked before and 3 after the pin (Fig 86). Make the 3 leaves *A*, *B* and *C*. Use each pair of bobbins as one thread and proceed as follows (Fig 86b).

1. Pass the left of the centre pairs under the next pair to the left.
2. Take the right pair of the centre pairs over the next pair to the right.
3. Twist once the 2 centre pairs, right over left.
4. Pass the left of the centre pairs out to the left under and over the next 2 pairs.
5. Take the right of the centre pairs out to the right over and under the next 2 pairs.
6. Put up a pin in the centre to keep pairs steady.
7. Repeat movements 1, 2 and 3.
8. Pass the left of the centre pairs under the next pair to the left.
9. Take the right centre pair over the next pair to the right.
10. Ease up carefully into position. Use the bobbins again singly and make the leaves *D*, *E* and *F*.

Note 12. Eight-pair crossing

Four leaves are worked before and 4 after the pin (Fig 87). Make the 4 leaves A, B, C and D. Use each pair of bobbins as one thread and work as follows.

1. Make a half-stitch with the centre 4 pairs.
2. Work a half-stitch with the right-hand 4 pairs.
3. Work a half-stitch with the left-hand 4 pairs.
4. Repeat these 3 half-stitches.
5. Put up a pin to keep all steady.
6. Work a whole stitch with the centre 4 pairs.
   Of the right-hand 4 pairs, cross the centre 2 – left over right.
   Of the left-hand 4 pairs, cross the centre 2 – left over right.
7. Ease up carefully into position.
8. Use the bobbins again singly and make the leaves E, F, G and H.

SETTING IN NEW PAIRS INTO THE TRAIL OR FOOTSIDE
Note 13. Setting in one or two new pairs

a. Setting in/working one new pair on the right (Fig 88)

An example of this is shown at pins marked *x* (Fig 88a). Work as follows.

Hang the new pair on a temporary pin above pin *x* (Fig 88b). Bring the weaver pair through the passive pairs towards pin *x*. Work it also through the new pair on the temporary pin. Put up pin *x* between the weaver pair and the new pair. Enclose pin *x* with the weaver pair and take the weaver pair on through the passives to pin 4. When working back to pin 5 the weaver pair works through all the pairs except the new one. This pair remains out of the trail at pin *x* to work another part of the design. Remove the temporary pin and pull this pair down into the lace.

b. Setting in/working 2 new pairs into one pin-hole (Fig 89)

i. Setting in 2 new pairs on the left of the trail or footside. In Bedfordshire lace these pairs are used to make a plait or a leaf. The method is used to set in: ninepin plait pairs into the trail, and ground plait or leaf pairs into the footside.

At the trail. Two pairs are needed to work the ninepin from pin A of the trail (see Fig 89a). Work as follows.

Hang 2 pairs open (N8) round temporary pin T above pin A (Fig 89b). Bring the trail weaver pair through the passives from pin 3 to pin A. Work the weaver pair on in whole stitch through the 2 new pairs on pin T.

Leave the weaver pair here, on the left of pin A. Set pin A between the 2 new pairs from pin T. Enclose pin A with the left-hand of these 2 pairs by taking it as the new weaver pair in whole stitch through the right-hand new pair and on through the trail passive pairs to pin 4.

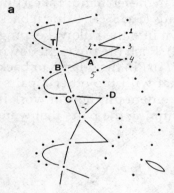

a

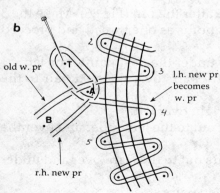

b

old w. pr

l.h. new pr
becomes
w. pr

r.h. new pr

Figure 89
Setting in new pairs into one pin-hole on the left of trail or footside.

a. Pattern section.
b. Working diagram.

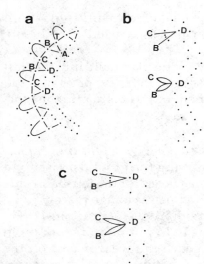

a

b

c

Figure 90
Working plait or leaf pairs into one pin-hole on the left of trail or footside where they leave immediately on the same side.
a. Ninepin joins outer trail.
b. Plaits/leaves from ground meet a centre trail.
c. Plaits/leaves from ground meet footside.

Twist the weaver pair once and put up pin 4 to the left of it. Remove the temporary pin *T* and ease the threads down into place round pin *A*. The 'old' weaver pair and the right-hand new pair remain out at pin *A* and make the plait to pin *B*.

Note. Do not remove the temporary pin before pin 4 is set as the new weaver pair is rather 'loose' until it has worked across the trail passives and is anchored by the pin on the other side of the trail. Remove immediately after setting pin 4, easing the pairs down into the lace. The new weaver pair needs to be eased across the trail.

ii. Working 2 plait or leaf pairs into one pin-hole on the left of the trail or footside, leaving immediately on the same side. In the examples shown in Fig 90 these pairs enter and are left out at pin *D*. The working is the same as for setting in 2 new pairs in Note 13b.i.

The plait or leaf pairs from pin *C* meet the trail at pin *D* (see Fig 91). Bring the weaver pair to pin *D* and work on in whole stitch through the 2 pairs of the plait or leaf. Leave the weaver pair to the left-hand side of pin *D*. Put up pin *D* between the 2 pairs of the plait (or leaf). Enclose pin *D* with the left-hand plait pair and take it as the new weaver pair in the trail, working in whole stitch through the right-hand plait pair and on through the passive pairs.

The 'old' weaver pair and the 'old' right-hand plait pair make the next plait (or leaf) from pin *D* to pin *B*.

At the footside. Two new pairs are set into the footside, and plait or leaf pairs are worked in and out of it, in the same way as for the trail above (N13b.i–ii) with one difference: after the weaver pair has worked through the footside passive pairs it is twisted once, before working through the 2 pairs of the plait or leaf, Fig 92b (or the new pairs, if setting in, Fig 92a).

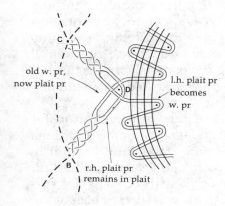

old w. pr, now plait pr

l.h. plait pr becomes w. pr

r.h. plait pr remains in plait

Figure 91
Detail of Figure 90a.

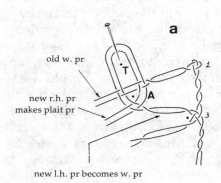

a

old w. pr

new r.h. pr makes plait pr

new l.h. pr becomes w. pr

Figure 92
a. Setting in 2 new pairs into one pin-hole on the left of footside.

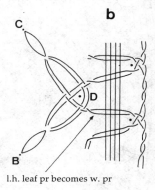

b

l.h. leaf pr becomes w. pr

b. Working 2 leaf/plait pairs into one pin-hole on left of footside, leaving immediately on the same side.

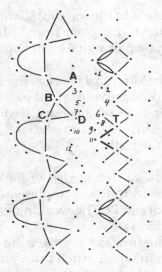

Figure 93
Setting in 2 new pairs into one pin-hole
on the right of the trail.

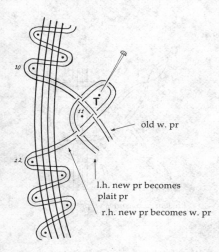

old w. pr

l.h. new pr becomes
plait pr

r.h. new pr becomes w. pr

Figure 94
Detail for Figure 93.

After enclosing pin *D* (Fig 92b) with the plait or leaf pairs (pin *A* with the new pairs, Fig 92a) the new weaver pair is twisted once before working on through the passive pairs.

Follow Pattern 4, ★★★ to ★★★, p. 22, for working plait pairs into the trail at pin *D*. See Pattern 6, ● to ● p. 28, for setting in 2 new pairs into the footside, and ★★ to ★★ p. 29 for working plait or leaf pairs into the foot-side.

iii. Setting in 2 new pairs into one pin-hole on the right of the trail or foot-side (Fig 93). Pairs of plaits and leaves working the ground are set into the trail on the right-hand side in the same way as for the left-hand side (see N13b.i above) except that right and left pairs change places.

Hang the 2 new pairs open round temporary pin *T* near pin *11* (Fig 94). Bring the trail weaver pair from pin *10* to pin *11* and work on in whole stitch through the 2 new pairs. Leave the weaver pair on the right-hand side of pin *11*. Put up pin *11* between the 2 new pairs. Enclose pin *11* with the right-hand new pair and take it as the new weaver pair for the trail, working whole stitch through the left-hand new pair and on through the trail passive pairs to pin *12*.

Twist the weaver pair once and put up pin *12* to the right of it. When the weaver pair is thus anchored remove the temporary pin and ease the 2 new pairs down into the lace.

The 'old' weaver pair and the new left-hand pair remain at pin *11* to make the plait (or leaf) see Fig 94.

iv. Working 2 plait or leaf pairs into one pin-hole, on the right of the trail, leaving immediately on the same side. In the example shown in Fig 95 the leaf pairs enter the trail from the ground at pin *11*. The working is the same as setting in 2 new pairs (N13b.iii).

Bring the weaver pair to pin *11* and work it in whole stitch through the 2 pairs of the plait (or leaf). Leave the weaver pair to the right of pin *11* and put up pin *11* between the plait pairs. Enclose pin *11* with the right-hand plait pair and take it as the new weaver pair in the trail, working in whole stitch through the left-hand plait pair and on through the trail passive pairs. The 'old' weaver pair and the 'old' left-hand plait pair remain at pin *11* to make the next plait.

If these procedures for taking plait and leaf pairs into the trail are followed, the lace will lie flat and have a neat appearance. Some traditional Bedfordshire lace-makers prefer to take both pairs into the trail by working the weaver pair through both pairs and setting the trail pin between the weaver pair and last pair worked through. They then enclose the pin in the normal way by taking the weaver pair back across the trail through all the pairs. Two pairs are then left out to make the next plait or leaf. This method does not, however, leave the lace with quite such a neat appearance.

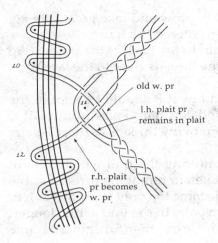

Figure 95
Working pairs on the right of the trail where they leave immediately on the same side.

Figure 95 labels:
- old w. pr
- l.h. plait pr remains in plait
- r.h. plait pr becomes w. pr.

WORKING PLAIT OR LEAF PAIRS INTO THE TRAIL OR FOOTSIDE; REMOVING THREADS

Note 14. Working plait or leaf pairs into the trail (or footside) which do not leave immediately

Treat the 2 pairs of the plait or leaf as if they were only one pair; that is, use 2 threads as one (Fig 96a). Take the weaver pair through the threads in whole stitch. Put up pin. Treat the 2 pairs now as separate pairs and in enclosing the pin work through each pair singly as passive pairs.

If the pairs are to leave the trail again fairly soon, they can remain in it as passive pairs until they are left out again. Leave 2 pairs out at the appropriate pin-hole after it has been enclosed by taking the weaver pair back across the trail.

This is what often shows in old Bedfordshire lace as a thicker part of the trail and it becomes distinctly thinner where the pairs leave again. It may be possible to move the trail pin-holes in a fraction, at the thinner parts, so that the effect shows less.

If the pairs are not leaving for some time, and especially if there are further pairs to be taken into the trail in the same way, it is often best to remove some threads from the trail and hang in new pairs again where needed. This will prevent the trail from becoming too bulky. Follow Note 15 for removing threads.

If the pin-holes of the trail are very close to each other the 2 pairs can be taken into the trail separately. One pair is taken in at each of 2 adjacent pin-holes (Fig 96b). They can be left out of the trail in the same way, at 2 adjacent pin-holes. Working in this way does prevent the 'bulk' caused by taking in 2 pairs at one pin-hole. Leaving the pairs out at 2 separate pin-holes makes a change in the number of passive pairs in the trail look less abrupt.

Note 15. Removing threads from a trail

Trails can become very bulky when plait or leaf pairs are taken in and do not leave for some time because they make extra passive pairs. When completing a piece of lace there may be plait or leaf pairs to come into the trail which then make too many pairs to fasten off into the available loops.

In order to accommodate the extra pairs and at the same time maintain the original number of passive pairs in the trail, the 2 threads of a pair can be removed. There is no set pattern to maintain the original number of threads but the following method is suggested as having the least risk of leaving a 'hole' where the extra threads are removed (Fig 97a).

The threads removed should be from pairs which have worked longest in the trail and *not* from those which have been recently added. Do *not* remove threads from the outer pairs but choose pairs from the

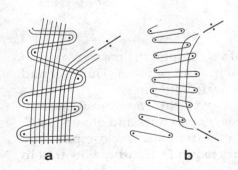

Figure 96
Taking plait or leaf pairs into the trail which do not leave immediately.
a. Both pairs taken in at same pin-hole.
b. Pairs taken in and left out at two adjacent pin-holes.

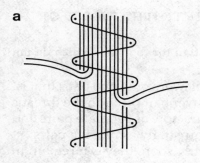

a

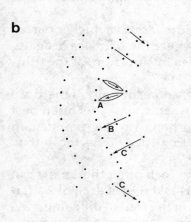

b

Figure 97
Removing extra threads from the trail.

centre. Remove only one pair per working row and take great care *not to remove* a pair which has only recently entered the trail.

Lift the bobbins of a pair and lay them to the back of the pillow (Fig 97a). The bobbins can be cut off. Trim the threads close to the lace later, when you have removed the pins.

Refer to Fig 97b. Pairs from leaf A and plait B should be kept in the trail and threads removed to accommodate them. Pairs from plait C could well be accommodated without removing threads as these 2 pairs will soon leave the trail.

If there are several plaits or leaves entering the trail which are not leaving for some time, care should be taken in removing threads as the recently added pairs can very quickly become the only alternatives left. In this case it is better to retain the extra pairs in the trail a little longer. This applies particularly to trails which have less than 5 original passive pairs.

Note 16. Working plait or leaf pairs 'through' a trail

Sometimes plait or leaf pairs enter a trail on one side and need to be left out again on the opposite side to work another plait or leaf. The following method is a very neat way of taking pairs 'through' the trail but will only work where the pairs are leaving on one side immediately above the point where the pairs are entering on the other side. In patterns where plait or leaf pairs do not quite fit this method, it is worth looking to see if slight alterations to the positioning of the plaits or leaves can be made to enable them to be taken through the trail in this way. Of course, this will not always be possible.

Take the trail weaver pair to pin A – twist it once – put up pin A. Do not enclose pin A – leave the weaver pair behind it.

Make the plait or leaf to pin B – set pin B between the plait or leaf pairs.

a. Working to the right (Fig 98a)

Work the right-hand plait pair from pin B through the passive pairs to pin A. Twist this pair once and leave it in front of pin A. This pair and the 'old' weaver pair make the plait (or leaf) from pin A.

Take the left-hand plait pair as the weaver pair from pin B through the passive pairs to pin C. Twist the weaver pair once and put up pin C. Retain this pair as the weaver pair in the trail and enclose pin C by working back through the passive pairs to pin D. Continue the trail in the usual way.

b. Working to the left (Fig 98b)

Work the left-hand pair from pin B through the passive pairs to pin A. Twist this pair once and leave it in front of pin A. This pair and the 'old'

a

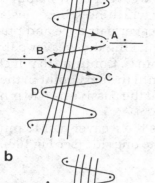

b

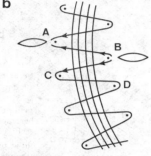

Figure 98
Taking plait or leaf pairs through the trail.
a. To the right.
b. To the left.

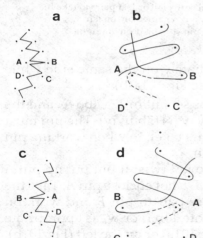

Figure 99
Gaining on a pin in the trail.
No plait or leaf pairs to take in.
a-b. Point in the trail on the right; pin A to be gained on, on the left.
c-d. Point in the trail on the left; pin A to be gained on, on the right.

weaver pair make the plait (or leaf) from pin A.

Take the right-hand plait (or leaf) pair as the new weaver pair from pin B through the passive pairs to pin C – twist it once – put up pin C. Retain this pair as the weaver pair – enclose pin C; continue to pin D as before.

OTHER TECHNIQUES

Note 17. Gaining on a pin in the trail

The trails in Bedfordshire lace are usually curved and some have very sharp bends or even points. There will be only one pin-hole on the inner side of the sharp bend but several on the opposite side (see Fig 99a, c). The single inner pin-hole will be worked into more than once and this procedure is called 'gaining on a pin'.

Care and judgement need to be used when gaining on a pin as the lace can begin to pucker instead of lying flat, especially if the pin has to be *gained on* more than once i.e. using it up to 3 times. As a general rule it is best to use a single pin-hole twice only. If this does not take the trail out of the point, gain on the next pin too, if this is possible, rather than use the pin-hole 3 times. This will prevent the work from puckering. Plait or leaf pairs from the ground often connect to the trail at these points and these connections have to be made neatly so that the lace will lie flat.

There are many ways to do this and some are given here. With experience the lace-maker can experiment when connecting plaits or leaves to trails, while also gaining on a pin, and find ways of giving the best appearance to the lace.

In order to gain on trail pins and to connect the plait or leaf pairs into the points, there will be a change in the use of the pairs being worked. Passive pairs will become weaver pairs – weaver pairs will become passives; plait or leaf pairs will become passive pairs and passives will become plait or leaf pairs.

The method used to gain on a pin will depend on the number and positions of pin-holes at the points where the lace needs to gain.

a. Gaining on a pin with no plaits or leaf pairs to take in

Figure 99a-c shows that the weaver pair cannot work from pin A to B and then from B to D. The weaver pair in the trail would first have to work forward one pin, then back one pin and so forth, instead of working continuously forward. Pin-hole A is therefore used twice – it is gained on.

Bring the weaver pair to pin A – do not twist it but put up pin A and leave the weaver pair here, behind pin A. Do not enclose pin A. Take the pair of passives lying next to pin A as the weaver pair to pin B (see Fig 99b-d). Twist once and put up pin B. This passive pair now remains as

17

the weaver pair. Bring this pair back to pin *A* through the passive pairs; this encloses pin *B*. Remove pin *A* and take the weaver pair from pin *B* in whole stitch through the 'old' weaver pair, which now becomes a passive pair (see Fig 100a-b). Twist the new weaver pair once and put up pin *A* again. This time pin *A* is enclosed by taking the weaver pair across the trail to pin *C*. Twist it once – put up pin *C*. Continue to pin *D* and on through the trail, working the pattern until the next point in the trail. At this point the weaver pair will be left and the passive next to pin *A* will become the new weaver pair as above.

Take care not to pull the passive pair used as the weaver pair to pin *B* too tightly, or the trail can be pulled markedly to one side (see Fig 100).

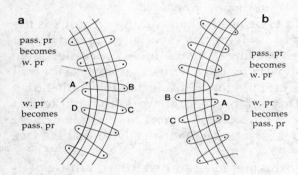

Figure 100
Details for Figure 99.
a. Detail for Figure 99a-b.
b. Detail for Figure 99c-d.

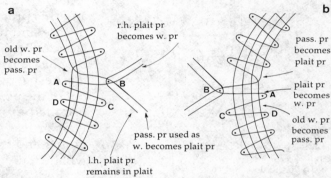

Figure 101
Gaining on a pin in the trail with plait or leaf pairs to take in.
a. Point and plait on right, pin *A* gained on, on left.
b. Point and plait on left, pin *A* gained on, on right.

b. Gaining on a pin with plait or leaf pairs to take in

Here the plait or leaf pairs leave immediately on the same side while gaining on a pin on the opposite side (see Fig 101a-b).

i. Method I. The pin can be gained on as set out in 17a above, and the plait or leaf pairs taken up in the usual way (N13b.ii, iv). The pin must be gained on first and the plait or leaf pairs taken in when working pin *B* with the passive pair as the weaver pair.

Take the trail weaver pair to pin *A*. Do not twist it but put up pin *A* and leave the weaver pair here behind it. Do not enclose pin *A*. Take the passive pair next to pin *A* as the weaver pair to pin *B* and work on through the plait or leaf pairs. Follow Note 13b.ii or iv, as appropriate to take in the plait pairs on the right (Fig 101a) or on the left (Fig 101b). Bring the new weaver pair to pin *A* from pin *B*. Remove pin *A* and work whole stitch through the 'old' weaver pair. Twist the new weaver pair once and put up pin *A* again. Bring the weaver pair to pin *C* and continue working the trail in the usual way. The passive pair from pin *A*, used as the weaver pair to pin *B*, is left out at pin *B* with a previous plait pair, to make the next plait.

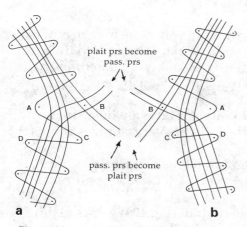

a   **b**

Figure 102
Gaining on a pin in the trail.
a. Plait enters trail on the right.
b. Plait enters trail on the left.

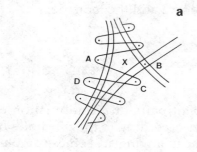

a

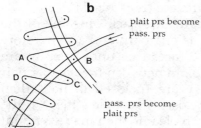

b

Figure 103
Gaining on a pin in the trail, with only
2 passive pairs in the trail.
a. When worked with more than 2
passive pairs a 'hole' may form at *x*.

ii. Method II (Fig 102a-b). This method is probably better when there are 4 or more passive pairs in the trail, as pin *A* does not have to be used more then once. The plait or leaf pairs change places with 2 passive pairs from the trail.

Plait enters on the right, Fig 102a. Take the weaver pair to pin *A* – twist it once and put up pin *A*. Leave the weaver pair here, behind pin *A*. Do not enclose pin *A*. Take the left-hand pair from the plait through all the trail passive pairs and leave it in the trail on the left-hand side, in front of pin *A*.

Set pin *B* between the 2 right-hand passive pairs of the trail. These 2 pairs will be left out at pin *B* to make the next plait or leaf.

Bring the right-hand pair from the plait through these 2 pairs and work on through the trail passive pairs so that it becomes the third passive from the left in the trail. This pair works in front of pin *B* and so encloses that pin.

Bring the weaver pair left at pin *A* in front of pin *A* and work it through the passive pairs to pin *C*. Continue the trail in the usual way.

Plait enters on the left. If the plait or leaf is taken in on the left-hand side, the weaver pair remains at pin *A*, as above (Fig 102b). The right-hand pair from the plait works through all the trail passives and stays as a passive pair on the right of the trail, in front of pin *A*. Pin *B* is put up between the 2 left-hand passive pairs of the trail and these form the next plait. The left-hand plait pair works through these 2 pairs and on through the trail passive pairs to become the third passive pair from the right. The weaver pair encloses pin *A* and works on to pin *C*.

This method has been used in Pattern 8 but Method I (N17b.i) could also be used.

c. Gaining on a pin with only 2 passive pairs in the trail

The method given here: changing passive pairs into plait pairs and plait pairs into passive pairs, can be used instead of the more elaborate methods described in 17b.i-ii above, but it can give the appearance of a 'hole' in the trail when there are more than 2 passive pairs in it. Its use in that instance would depend on the position of the pin-holes and the sharpness of the curve (see *x* on Fig 103a).

The following method, when used with only 2 pairs of passives in the trail, gives a very neat appearance to the lace (Fig 103b).

Work to pin *A* – twist the trail weaver pair once. Put up pin *A* and leave the weaver pair behind it, without enclosing the pin.

Work the plait to pin *B* and take the left-hand plait pair through the 2 passives of the trail in whole stitch. Put up pin *B* between the 2 passive pairs. Bring the right-hand plait pair in front of pin *B* and work it in whole stitch through the 2 passive pairs. This encloses pin *B*.

The 2 passive pairs remain out at pin *B* to form the next plait and the 2 previous plait pairs become the passive pairs in the trail. Enclose pin *A* by bringing the weaver pair through the new passive pairs to pin *C*.

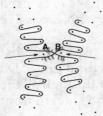

a

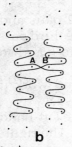

b

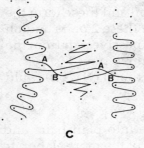

c

Figure 104
Parts of the lace where a 'kiss' is required.
a. Two trails meet.
b. Trail and footside meet.
c. Trail, circle and footside.

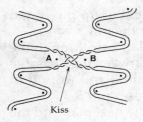

Kiss

Figure 105
Kiss.

Note 18. The 'kiss'

When there are 2 trails in a pattern which are very close to each other at certain pin-holes (Fig 104a), or if the trail works very close to the foot-side (Fig 104b), the 2 are joined together by a 'kiss'. Sometimes half-stitch circles may be joined to the trail or the footside by working a kiss at the centre pin-holes of the circle (Fig 104c).

The kiss is made by the 2 weaver pairs working a whole stitch and changing places, for example when the trails are very close, as at pins A and B in Fig 105.

The trail weaver pair in the left-hand trail (Fig 105) works to pin A, is twisted several times and then pin A is set. This weaver pair remains behind pin A which is not enclosed.

The trail weaver pair in the right-hand trail (Fig 105) works to pin B; it is twisted several times and pin B is set. This weaver pair is left behind pin B which is not enclosed. The 2 weaver pairs now work a whole stitch and change places. They are both twisted several times.

The left-hand weaver pair (which came from the right-hand trail) works back into the left-hand trail, enclosing pin A as it works in front of it.

The right-hand weaver pair (which came from the left-hand trail) works back into the right-hand trail, enclosing pin B as it works in front of it.

The number of twists on the weaver pairs depends on the thread size and the 'gap' between the 2 trails, or the trail and the footside.

Note 19. Half-stitch circles

Description and general points

The circles are made from leaf pairs, plait pairs or a combination of both. They can be begun in several ways according to the pin-holes of the circle and the pairs coming into it. The following are some examples of half-stitch circles found in Bedfordshire lace (Figs 106-110).

Although 2 pairs are very often brought into each pin-hole of the circle the 2 pairs are treated singly, not as one pair, and are therefore worked through separately. *Do not* treat 2 threads as one. The pins are enclosed in the usual way by putting the pin between the weaver pair and the last pair worked through. They are enclosed in half-stitch except the last one, which should be enclosed in whole stitch – if the pairs left out from it are to make a leaf. The leaf is then made without working a further whole stitch to begin it.

In some circles there may be pin-holes at which no pairs enter or leave. These pins are worked as the circle progresses by taking the weaver pair round them in half-stitch and working back to the other side.

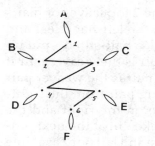

Figure 106
Half-stitch circle with 6 leaves or plaits.

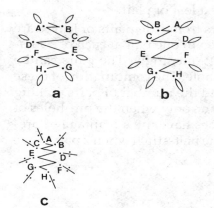

Figure 107
Half-stitch circle with 8 leaves or plaits.
a. Method i. b. Method ii. c. Method iii.

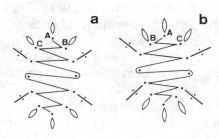

Figure 108
Half-stitch circles with other number of leaves or plaits.
a. Right-hand pair becomes weaver pair after enclosing pin *A*.
b. Left-hand pair becomes weaver pair after enclosing pin *A*.

a. Half-stitch circles with 6 leaves or plaits

In this case 3 leaves or plaits enter the circles and 3 are left out (Fig 106).

Finish the top leaf *A* with a whole stitch and then put up pin *1* between the 2 pairs of the leaf. Enclose the pin with half-stitch and work in half-stitch through the 2 pairs of leaf *B*. Put up pin 2 between the weaver pair and the last pair worked through. Bring the weaver pair back through the pairs in half-stitch, including the 2 pairs of leaf *C*. Put up pin 3. Enclose the pin and work to pin 4. Leave 2 pairs out at pin 4. Take the weaver pair back through all the pairs to pin 5. Leave 2 pairs out at pin 5. Work through the remaining pairs to pin 6. Enclose pin 6 with the last 2 pairs and leave these out at pin 6.

b. Half-stitch circles with 8 leaves or plaits

In this case 4 leaves or plaits enter the circle and 4 are left out (Fig 107a-c). Methods I and II can be used when there are not many pairs coming into the circle and the circle is fairly large because it gives an extra row of half-stitch.

i. Method I. Follow Fig 107a. Take the right-hand pair from *A* in half-stitch through the 2 pairs at *B*. Put up pin *B* between the weaver pair and the last pair worked through. Work back to *A* in half-stitch and take up the left-hand pair from *A*. Put up pin *A*. Work to pins *C* and *D* taking in 2 pairs at each pin. Work pins *E*, *F*, *G* and *H*, leaving 2 pairs out at each pin after enclosing them.

ii. Method II. Follow Fig 107b. Working from the right-hand side, begin with the left-hand pair from *A*. Work to *B* and take in the 2 pairs. Put up pin *B* and work back to *A* – take in the right-hand pair from *A* and put up the pin. Take in 2 pairs at each of the pins *C* and *D* and leave out 2 pairs at each of the pins *E*, *F*, *G* and *H* after enclosing the pins.

iii. Method III. Follow Fig 107c. If the circle is small use Note 19a above. Take in 2 pairs at *A* and each of the other pin-holes *B*, *C* and *D* and leave out 2 pairs at each pin-hole *D*, *F*, *G* and *H*.

c. Half-stitch circles with other numbers of leaves or plaits

i. Method I. Fig 108. Put up pin *A* between the 2 pairs of the *top leaf* and enclose it with a half-stitch. Take the remaining pairs in, two at each pin-hole, beginning either on the right or the left. If the first 2 pairs are taken in on the right then the weaver pair is the right-hand pair from pin *A* (Fig 108a). If the first 2 pairs are taken in on the left then the weaver pair is the left-hand pair from *A* (Fig 108b).

The pairs are left out, 2 at each appropriate pin-hole, after enclosing the pins, the last 2 pairs making and enclosing the last pin-hole at the bottom of the circle.

At pin-holes where no pairs enter or leave, take the weaver pair round the pins in half-stitch and across to the other side of the circle.

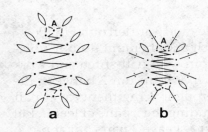

Figure 109
Half-stitch circles.
a. One pair from each of 2 top leaves
begin the circle.
b. One pair from each of two top plaits
begin the circle.

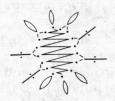

Figure 110
Half-stitch circle.
Side pairs taken in singly.

ii. Method II. Fig 109. One pair from each of the 2 top leaves or plaits begin the circle. With the right-hand pair from the left-hand leaf and the left-hand pair from the right-hand leaf, work a half-stitch – put up pin A – enclose in half-stitch. The right-hand pair is the weaver pair if you are working to the right first; the left-hand pair is the weaver pair if you are working to the left first. The remaining pair from the right-hand leaf/plait is taken in at the next pin-hole on the right and the remaining pair from the left-hand leaf/plait is taken in at the next pin-hole on the left. Other pairs are taken in 2 at a time and left out 2 at a time at the appropriate pin-holes.

The last 3 pin-holes work as the first three. One pair is left out on the left-hand side, one pair on the right and the last 2 pairs from the last pin-hole. These 2 pairs then work one to the right and one to the left to join with the single pairs to make the next leaf or plait.

iii. Method III. Fig 110. Sometimes pairs from side plaits or leaves are taken into the circle singly. They are taken in one pair at each of 2 adjacent pin-holes. The pairs can also be left out singly. The pairs can be *taken in* singly, and left out 2 at each pin-hole. The combination of these procedures depends on the pin-holes and the number of pairs. Taking in and leaving out single pairs is best done only when the pin-holes of the circle are very close together, but does have the advantage of preventing the 'gaps' which can appear in the half-stitch when 2 pairs have been left out at the same pin-hole.

Note 20. Crossing trails (in the form of an X)

a. Crossing trails where no pairs are taken in at pin A.

Take the trail weaver pair from pin *a* on the left, through the passive pairs to pin *A* in the centre of the crossing (Fig 111). Twist it once. Take the trail weaver pair from pin *b* on the right through the passive pairs to pin *A*. Twist it once. Work a whole stitch with the two weaver pairs. Put up pin *A* between them. Work a whole stitch with them to enclose pin *A*. Do not twist them.

Bring the left-hand pair as the weaver pair through the left-hand passive pairs to pin *B*. Twist it once and put up pin *B*. Leave the weaver pair behind pin *B*. Do not enclose it.

Take the right-hand pair from pin *A* as the weaver pair through the right-hand passive pairs to pin *C*. Twist it once and put up pin *C*. Leave the weaver pair behind pin *C*. Do not enclose it.

Work the passive pairs through each other in whole stitch. This crosses them over. The original left-hand side passive pairs from between pins *A* and *B* now lie on the right between pins *C* and *D*. The orginal right-hand passive pairs from between pins *A* and *C* now lie on the left, between pins *B* and *D*. After crossing the passive pairs, the weaver pairs enclose pins *B* and *C* by working to pin *D*.

Bring the weaver pair from pin *B* through the new left-hand passive pairs to pin *D*. Bring the weaver from pin *C* through the new right-hand passive pairs to pin *D*. Do not twist the weaver pairs.

Work a whole stitch with the 2 weaver pairs. Put up pin *D* between them and enclose pin *D* with the 2 weaver pairs in whole stitch. Do not twist them. Take the left-hand pair from pin *D* to pin *c* in whole stitch through the left-hand passive pairs. It remains in the left-hand trail as the weaver pair.

Take the right-hand pair from pin *D* to pin *d* in whole stitch through the right-hand passive pairs. It remains in the right-hand trail as the weaver pair.

The trails continue separately until the next crossing.

Note: A little thought must be given to trails before crossing them if extra pairs have been accumulated into them from plaits or leaves.

While it may be possible to carry the extra pairs in the normally worked trail, it is not always a good idea to carry extra pairs through the crossing. They can make it look rather bulky. It is better to remove extra pairs before working the crossing and add new pairs later as required. This is a matter for the individual lace-maker to decide when working a particular pattern.

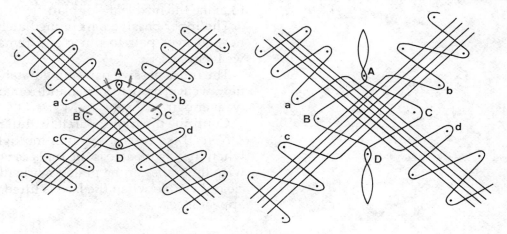

Figure 111
Crossing trails.
No pairs are taken in at pin *A*.

Figure 112
Crossing trails.
Plait or leaf pairs join the trail at pin *A*.

b. Crossing trails where a plait or leaf enters the trail at pin A (as in Fig 112)

An example of this is worked in Pattern 12, p. 58.

Follow Fig 112. Take the weaver pair from pin *a* in the left-hand trail to pin *A*. Leave it in front of pin *A* as a passive pair on the right-hand side of this trail, lying next to pin *A*. *Do not twist it.*

Work the weaver pair from pin *b* in the right-hand trail to pin *A*.

Leave it in front of pin *A* as a passive pair on the left-hand side of this trail, lying next to pin *A*. *Do not twist it.*

Put up pin *A* between the leaf (or plait) pairs. Enclose pin *A* with the leaf pairs in whole stitch. *Do not* twist these pairs.

Take the left-hand pair from pin *A* as the weaver pair through the left-hand passive pairs to pin *B*. The passive pairs now include the 'old' weaver pair from pin *a*. Twist the new weaver pair once – put up pin *B* and leave this pair behind pin *B*. Do not enclose pin *B*.

Work the right-hand pair from pin *A* as the weaver pair through the right-hand passive pairs to pin *C*. The passive pairs now include the 'old' weaver pair from pin *b*. Twist the new weaver pair once – put up pin *C* and leave this pair behind pin *C*. Do not enclose pin *C*.

Work the trail passive pairs through each other in whole stitch. This crosses them over, the original left-hand pairs now lying on the right and original right-hand pairs lying on the left.

Bring the weaver pair from pin *B* through the new left-hand passive pairs to pin *D*. Do not twist it. Work the weaver pair from pin *C* through the new right-hand passive pairs to pin *D*. Do not twist it. Bringing these 2 pairs to pin *D* encloses pins *B* and *C*.

Work a whole stitch with the 2 weaver pairs – put up pin *D* and work a whole stitch with them to enclose pin *D*. Leave these 2 pairs at pin *D* to make the next leaf – or plait.

The inner passive pair immediately to the left of pin *D* becomes the new weaver pair to pin *c* and remains in the left-hand trail as the weaver pair.

The inner passive pair immediately to the right of pin *D* becomes the new weaver pair to pin *d* and remains in the right-hand trail as the weaver pair.

Continue the trail separately until the next crossing.

Note: Take care not to pull too tightly on the 2 inner passive pairs when they work across the trails as weaver pairs to pins *c* and *d*, otherwise the trails can be pulled markedly to the right or left. This will be clearly visible when the lace is lifted from the pillow and will spoil its appearance.

Other Lace, Costume and Embroidery Books

The Technique & Design of Cluny Lace L Paulis/Maria Rutgers
0 903585 18 9   220 × 174mm, 96p, 130ill, hardbound

Victorian Costume & Costume Accessories Anne Buck
0 903585 17 0   220 × 174mm, 224p, 90ill, paperback

Le Pompe 1559 Santina Levey/Pat Payne
(Patterns for Venetian Bobbin Lace)
0 903585 16 2   243 × 177mm, 128p, 97ill, paperback.

Teach Yourself Torchon Lace Eunice Arnold
0 903585 08 1   240 × 190mm, 40p, 6workcards, 27ill, limpbound

Pillow Lace – A Practical Hand-book E Mincoff/M Marriage
0 903585 10 3   216 × 138mm, 304p, 2worksheets, 90ill, hardbound

Victorian Lace Patricia Wardle
0 903585 13 8   222 × 141mm, 304p, 82pl, hardbound

Thomas Lester His Lace & E Midlands Industry 1820–1905 Anne Buck
0 903585 09 X   280 × 210mm, 120p, 55pl, hardbound

The Romance of the Lace Pillow Thomas Wright
0 903585 12 X   222 × 141mm, 340p, 50pl, hardbound

Tailor's Pattern Book 1589 Juan de Alcega
(Libro de Geometria, Pratica y Traça)
0 903585 06 5   279 × 203mm, 244p, 137ill, clothbound

In preparation

Embroidery in 18th Century Britain Patricia Wardle
0 903585 19 7   c.400p, 150ill

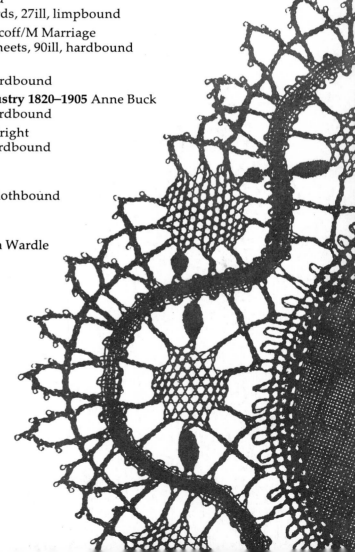

Books on Textiles from:

RUTH BEAN Publishers

VICTORIA FARMHOUSE
CARLTON
BEDFORD MK43 7LP
ENGLAND

A MANUAL OF BEDFORDSHIRE LACE

PAM ROBINSON

PART III

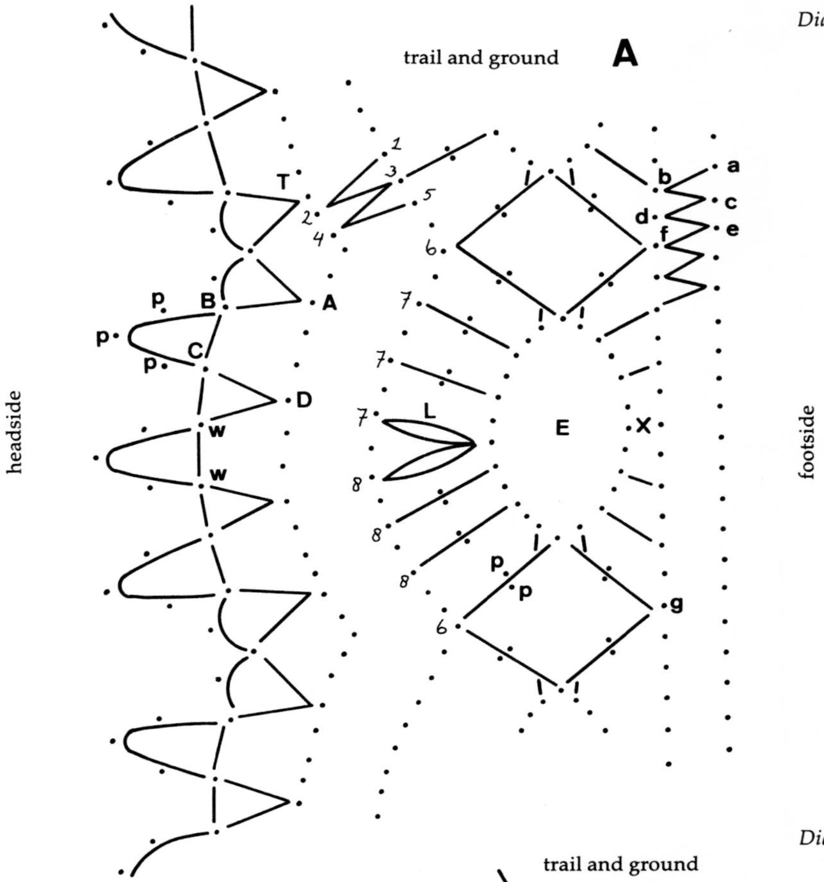

trail and ground **A**

headside

footside

T

1
3
2
4
5
6

b a
c
d e
f

p B A
p C
p D
w
w

7
7
7
8
8
8
6

L E X

p
p g

trail and ground **B**

headside

footside

w
w
w

F

9 10
10
9 8
11
12

10
9
11 9

9 10
9 10
11

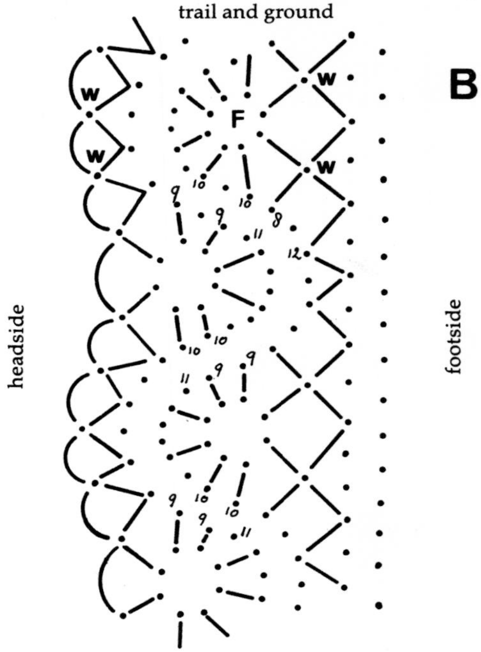

Two typical Bedfordshire patterns.